HOMELESS
NOT HELPLESS

An Anthology

Edited by

Barbara Paschke
&
David Volpendesta

CANTERBURY PRESS

CANTERBURY PRESS
P.O. Box 2151c
Berkeley, California 94702

Design: Canterbury Press
Design consultant: Sarah Levin
Cover design: Bob Baldock
Cover photograph: Al Harris Stein

Library of Congress Catalog Card: 88-72367
ISBN: 0933753-05-5

Printed in the United States of America

1 2 3 4 5 – 95 94 93 92 91

Acknowledgments

Steve Abbott's essay "On The Streets" first appeared in *The Sentinel*. Dan Bellm's article "AIDS/ARC and Homelessness" first appeared in *Coming-Up!*. A special acknowledgment to Geoff Froner, who provided the research upon which portions of this article are based. Jack Hirschman's poem "Home" first appeared in *The People's Tribune*. Maxine Hong Kingston's story "He be Santa" is from her best-selling novel, *Tripmaster Monkey*. A special acknowledgment and thanks to Alfred Knopf for permission to reprint. Portions of Daniel Lindley's "State Park Homeless" first appeared as a news story published by Pacific News Service. The radio play by Studs Terkel, *Home Sweet Home*, was later adapted under a script development grant from the Illinois Humanities Council and Illinois Arts Council. A special acknowledgment to Al Harris Stein, who provided the research and discovered this, among many other lost radio plays by Terkel, in the Illinois State Historical Library archives. In addition, another special acknowledgment to Al Stein, whose research uncovered Rajat Neogy's "Baby, It's Cold Outside" and Otis Thomas' "Oral History." For their extensive contributions on behalf of this book, the editors would like to extend a very special thanks to Bob Baldock, an artist, designer, and organizer; Jorge Argueta, a Salvadoran poet and performance artist; Sarah Menefee, a homeless activist and a member of Food Not Bombs; Joyce Jenkins, the editor/publisher of *Poetry Flash*; Stephen Kessler, former editor/publisher of the Santa Cruz weekly, *The Sun*; Chuy Varela of KPFA-FM; and Norine Brogan and Ian Faircloth of Canterbury Press.

Contents

Photographs
& Artwork

Introduction

During the last national census, newspapers and periodicals throughout the country pointed out that the homeless population had not been adequately counted. Not surprisingly, these vehicles of popular opinion —the majority of which are owned by fewer than thirty corporations— neglected to emphasize one basic fact: that the first people to be made homeless in this country were its original citizens, Native Americans. Homelessness has been with us since the beginning, only the stereotypes have changed.

In relation to mass popular consciousness, stereotypes are placebos that permit the viruses of prejudice and social injustice to multiply into an epidemic. Currently, the homeless are depicted as drunks, drug addicts, crazies, and socioeconomic parasites. The overall effect of these stereotypes has been to equate the homeless with being simultaneously worthless and helpless.

Reality, however, belies this inhumane equation. Not only have the homeless organized themselves into unions in several major cities in the country, but they have also taken the initiative to rehabilitate and occupy vacant federally owned housing developments.

On March 5, 1990, to cite a recent example, homeless people in Detroit and Philadelphia began one such occupation. Nathaniel Thomas, vice-president of the Detroit chapter of the Union of the Homeless, commented: "This is not an action…This is an ongoing campaign which will continue until Jack Kemp (Secretary of Housing and Urban Development) keeps his promise to give 10 percent of HUD's single-family properties to the homeless." (Kemp had made the promise five months earlier, on October 6, 1989.)

Four days later, as a result of these occupations, Mayor Coleman Young of Detroit met with the union. Saying that the meeting was the basis for an ongoing relationship, the mayor promised to send a staff member to inspect a model homeless housing project in Philadelphia and to begin a pilot homeless housing program in Detroit. He also said he would supply homes from the city's vacated single-family dwellings

1

as soon as the buildings that the homeless had already seized were rehabilitated.

In Philadelphia, where the local chapter of the Union of the Homeless first began occupying HUD buildings in 1988, the results of the March fifth occupation were similarly favorable. That city's mayor, W. Wilson Goode, said through a spokesperson that his administration supports the Homeless Union's efforts. And Ed Schwartz, Philadelphia Housing Commissioner, has stated: "During the Republican administration[s], housing has been treated as a commodity....We don't see public housing as an entrepreneurial opportunity."

In addition to housing, homeless people are also struggling for employment training and job placement services, as well as positions of responsibility in the development and management of homeless programs. These are not the types of pursuits people engage in if they perceive themselves as worthless and helpless.

This book affirms the human dignity and individual worth of those who are and have been forsaken, oppressed, and cast out. From Studs Terkel's radio play "Home Sweet Home" to Cecile Pineda's satirical essay "Payloads Into Caseloads: An Immodest Proposal," the photographs, short stories, poetry, articles, personal testimonies, essays, and artwork contained herein converge to explore the emotional dimensions and realities of the homeless. In the process of this exploration, these works—many by people who have been or who are now homeless—help to give a face and identity to the homeless who too often remain anonymous. We hope that this book can serve as an antidote to the stereotypes perpetuated by the present-day plague of North American poverty.

Barbara Paschke and David Volpendesta, editors
December 1990, San Francisco, California

Home Sweet Home

A Radio Play

Studs Terkel

MUSIC *"Home, Sweet Home"*

NARRATOR President Roosevelt, in his second inaugural address, spoke of the one-third of a Nation—*forty million people*—ill-clad, ill-fed, ill-housed. How do these people live? How did they get that way? *What makes for slums?*

WESTCOTT What makes for slums, eh? If you want my opinion, Miller, it's the people themselves. There's an old saying, 'dirt begets dirt'—if you know what I mean.

MILLER Yes, I know what you mean, Westcott—and, of course, I disagree with you heartily. My friend, when are you going to learn that it's *buildings* and *not people* that make slums?

WESTCOTT Now don't get sentimental on me, Miller.

MILLER I'm not—it's only a matter of common sense. Don't you think these people want clean, decent homes to live in, just as you and I?

WESTCOTT I wonder. You know, most of them have brought their habits and customs with them from the old country—and they're not the best in the world either.

MILLER Well, just suppose we take an actual district—our own slum area: Halsted Street—say, from Polk to about Twenty-second. You know, mostly foreigners live there. Let's find out how they live—why they came to Chicago in the first place. *(FADE)*

SOUND *Jabber of many voices; Sound of boat whistle*

BERGER Soon we be in America—then Chicago. [OVERWHELMED] Oh, Minnie—we'll be so happy. No more pogroms—no more hiding in cellars.

MINNIE [WITH EMOTION] I can't wait, Harry, I can't wait! Chicago. Jacob fixed it up with his boss—a job waiting for you in the dress factory.

BERGER You got a good brother, Minnie—a cutter's a good job— we're lucky. I'll never be able to pay him back.

MINNIE Don't be foolish—it makes him happy to do it. [SOFTLY] Think of it, Harry: our Sammy can go to school in Chicago— and maybe someday be a doctor or a lawyer...Dr. Samuel Berger.

BERGER I hope so. *(FADE)*

ROMANO Salvatore! Where is he go?

MARY [LAUGHS] Joseph. Don' holler. He's young boy—free— lively.

ROMANO Wild boy! Bad.

MARY He's good boy, Joseph. He—Carmella—bot' nice kids. You know it.

ROMANO [LAUGHS] Yeh. You right, Mary. I no holler no more. [IMPATIENTLY] But this such long trip—wish we are in Chicago *now*.

MARY [SOOTHINGLY] Soon, soon, Joseph Romano—we be in own home—Carmella an' Salvatore go to school—grow up good an' strong—me in nice kitchen wit' own sink, you have job—

ROMANO Yeh—I have good job soon. Marco is good friend— remember letter he wrote—

MARY Yes—he's got big grocery in Chicago—

ROMANO —on a place—Halsted—an' he's gon' give me horse an' wagon— [GAINING MOMENTUM] an' I go t'rough streets an' sing—*Apples—Bananas—*

MARY [LAUGHINGLY RESTRAINING HIM] Joseph—people looking at you—like crazy.

JOSEPH [QUIETER, but HAPPY] I no care how they look— [SUD-DENLY BURSTS OUT] *La Donna Mobile*— [LAUGHS] (FADE)

RODZINSKI How you feel, Sophie?

SOPHIE Wonderful, Anton.

RODZINSKI You want somet'ing to eat?

SOPHIE No, darling—I'm not hungry.

RODZINSKI You got eat a lot—must eat for two.

SOPHIE [LAUGHS SOFTLY] No, Anton. Don't worry—everyt'ing be all right.

RODZINSKI Sure—I get job in Chicago stockyards. They need big, strong man like me. Make lotsa money—good home—for you an' little one. How long gon' be now, Sophie?

SOPHIE Two months.

RODZINSKI Is gon' be boy or girl? Make it boy, Sophie. I wan' big, strong boy—jus' like father, Anton Rodzinski. Make it boy, Sophie.

SOPHIE If it be girl—you like her too. You better.

RODZINSKI [LAUGHS] Sure—sure. Boy or girl—he be American citizen—born in Chicago—Say! Maybe be president some day.

SOPHIE [SOFTLY] President. Don't be stupid. [BOTH LAUGH]

RODZINSKI Y'know—when I get job in stockyards—I send for everybody—my father, mother – brother – sister. Anton Rodzinski send for everybody! (FADE)

SOUND *Crowd noises mount; Whistles; Horns.*

VOICE I: America!

VOICE II: Look — Statue of Liberty!

MARY Salvatore! Carmella!

ANTON Look, Sophie!

SAMMY Pop—Mom— Statue of Liberty! [CHEERS]

SOUND *Noise: Crowd; Whistles; Horns reach crescendo.* (FADE)

MUSIC *"My Country, 'Tis of Thee"*

SOUND *Footsteps on rickety stairs—Door creaks open.*

LANDLORD This way, Mr. Berger. Here's the rooms.

BERGER Is this the rooms? *This* isn't what I expected.

LANDLORD [CURTLY] Well—you want three rooms, don't you. Here's three rooms—kitchen – bedroom – living room. Not the best in the world, but good enough. This is Halsted Street – not Prairie Avenue.

BERGER But it's so dark—no air.

MINNIE [AGHAST] The bedroom got no window.

LANDLORD Now just a minute. If you don't like it, say so. I can rent this place—one – two – three. Lotsa people coming into

Chicago these days—not many flats empty *now*—people just like you comin' in by the trainload. If you don't want these rooms just say so.

BERGER [QUICKLY] But we want them. We got to have some place to live.

SAMMY I'm tired, Pop.

BERGER Yeh, yeh, Sammy. How much did you say was the rent?

LANDLORD Twenty dollars a month.

BERGER Twenty dollars. Here's the money.

LANDLORD [COUNTING MONEY] That's right—twenty dollars. You know, Mr. Berger, you're lucky. I could get twenty-five dollars for this next week. Well—I guess you know where the water closet is—

BERGER Yes.

LANDLORD Well, good-bye.

SOUND *Door creaks as it is closed.*

MINNIE Where is the water closet, Harry?

BERGER I think he said it's in the hall downstairs.

MINNIE In the hall—downstairs! Sharing it with other families? And it's so cold in the hall.

SAMMY What's that smell, Mom?

MINNIE I don't know. It's all over.

SAMMY I don't like this place. It's so dark and damp. Can't even sit on the fire-escape and get fresh air. It's shaky.

BERGER Now, Sammy, don't holler. Don't worry—this is only for

7

now. Later—I get a better job—we move into a nice, clean place with our own water closet. *(FADE)*

SOUND *Chair scraping floor*

SALVATORE Aw, what's de use. I can't study here—too dark.

ROMANO Study, Salvatore.

SALVATORE I can't, Pop. Besides, it's cold here—an' dat smell— an' you holler because I didn't pass last time in school.

CARMELLA Pop, Salvatore's right. When are we going to move out of here—I'm sick of this place. The streets are so dark outside —no lights. I'm scared to go out alone. Can't even go for a walk in the park.

JOSEPH Carmella—I want move from here to nicer place. Bad street outside. My horse almost break leg. But we can't move now.

SOUND *Knock on door*

JOSEPH Come in.

SOUND *Door opens and closes*

JOSEPH Oh—hello – Mr. Landlord.

LANDLORD Hello, Mr. Romano.

ROMANO Today is rent day, hah?

LANDLORD That's right. Twenty-five dollars.

ROMANO Mr. Landlord—Could I give you twenty now and five dollar next week?

LANDLORD No sir. I'm sorry. You've got to pay rent when it's due.

ROMANO I jus' ask. Here's the money.

MARY [SOTTO VOCE] Joseph, tell him about ceiling.

ROMANO Yes. The plaster fall from ceiling in kitchen—maybe you fix it, hah?

LANDLORD Can't do that, Mr. Romano. I can't go to any extra expenses now. Not makin' any profit outa this building.

ROMANO I jus' ask.

LANDLORD Well, so long. I'll see you next month.

ROMANO Good-bye.

SOUND *Door opens and closes*

CARMELLA Pop—why do we live in this hole? He won't even fix anything. You pay him rent.

ROMANO Carmella—we got live some place. Other places too much money. Business very bad now.

MARY Joseph. Better tell children about Mike.

SALVATORE Mike who?

ROMANO Children—business is very bad. We got t'ree rooms here. You know what rent is. Twenty-five dollars is a lot money. Hard to pay. So next week we take in my friend, Mike Tolli, as boarder. He'll pay eight dollar month.

CARMELLA [BURSTING OUT] Pop—you can't do that. Five people in three room. I'll have no private place at all now. [SOBS]

ROMANO I'll hang a clothes up on line here—you have private.

CARMELLA [SOBBING] Where are we all gonna sleep? I'm no kid any more, Pop. I'm fifteen.

ROMANO [SADLY] I know, Bambina.

CARMELLA You don't know anything. [GOING OFF]

SOUND *Door slams*

MARY Joseph—does Mike Tolli gotta come live here?

ROMANO [BROKEN] Only for a little while, Mary— only for a little while. Why we fight—let's go for walk in park—get the sun – fresh air. *(FADE)*

SOUND *Door opens*

KLEPAK [HEARTY] Come in, Anton.

RODZINSKI Hello, John.

MRS. KLEPAK Hello, Sophie. How's the baby?

SOPHIE Fine, thanks. He had a little cold last week but he's better now.

MRS. KLEPACK Sit down here—in this chair; it's the softest one in the house.

KLEPAK It's the only good one. [BOTH LAUGH] Hello, baby— Anton, Junior, hah? Like his father.

RODZINSKI [BITTERLY] Hope he's not dumb like father.

KLEPAK Now – now, Anton. Waddaya mean—dumb? *You* can't help it—big layoff at yards—slack season now. So what—so you live with us 'til you get job.

SOPHIE But John, you've got a big family here yourself.

KLEPAK Big? No. Only t'ree kids—Catherine here and bulldog – Butch – sure, we got plenty room—three more won' hurt.

RODZINSKI [BITTER] I feel like dog—living on you.

KLEPAK Shut up, Anton. This is only for little while. Eight people —four rooms—not so bad —a little crowded, but not bad.

MRS. KLEPAK Sophie, maybe you and baby better wash up. Stanley —take pail with you. Go down yard—bring up water.

KLEPAK [JOVIALLY] Anton—I get some wine. Come—we drink to better times. *(FADES)*

SOUND *Horse and wagon on rough street; Children's voices— sound of hurdy-gurdy*

LITTLE BOY [CHANTING] Come out, come out, wherever you are.

BIG BOY [MIMICKING] Come out, come out, wherever you are. Hey, Ikey, what are you got in your pocket?

LITTLE BOY My name ain't Ikey.

BIG BOY It ain't, huh? Well, it's Ikey to me. Ya got candy in your pocket, aintcha.

LITTLE BOY No, I ain't. Honest.

BIG BOY Come on, ya little punk. Gimme de candy or I'll mobilize ya. Come on, gimma dat candy!

LITTLE BOY Lemme go, lemme go.

SOUND *Slap; thud; sobs.*

BIG BOY Dat'll learn ya, to get smart wit' me.

LITTLE BOY [SOBBING] I didn't do nuttin' to you.

BIG BOY [FADING] An' dat's jest a sample of what you'll get next time.

KILLEFER [LAUGHING INDULGENTLY] Say, he's a tough little monkey, isn't he, Dawson?

DAWSON   You said it. They don't come any tougher than the kids around here.

KILLEFER   Next thing you know they'll be toting guns.

DAWSON   You're telling me. Killefer – they're hoodlums all right. After all, what do ya expect—they're our criminal element— you know, foreigners—only kind you can get to live out here.

KILLEFER   Yeh – I know. By the way, I'm making the rounds today.

DAWSON   [LAUGHS] Oh – I had forgotten your job, *Inspector* Killefer.

KILLEFER   It's just a routine examination – for the department records, you know.

DAWSON   Do you want to go inside?

KILLEFER   Gosh, no. I can't stand the smell. Look – I'll take your word. Everything's in pretty good shape, isn't it?

DAWSON   Yeh, sure. I keep it okay – but you know these foreigners – they're pretty dirty.

KILLEFER   Yeh – I know – it's the same all over this neighborhood. Say – uh fumigate the toilet every now and then, willya – and don't let the garbage pile up too much in the cellar—you know, regulations.

DAWSON   Okay Killefer.

KILLEFER   Guess I'll mosey along.

DAWSON   Don't take any wooden nickels.

KILLEFER   I won't. I'm goin' to the ballgame—Giants in town – [FADING] Wouldn't miss it for anything – not even a fire.

SOUND   *Crackling of wood, paper – Hissing – Scream.*

VOICE Fire! Fire! [MORE SCREAMS]

SOUND *Sirens; Crowd noises – throughout*

WADE (Fireman) All right, all right, everybody—stand back.

SECOND FIREMAN Hey, Wade—shoot the hose all around the building—all these shacks are tinder heaps – heck of a job to keep this from spreading—

CHILD'S VOICE [AFAR] Help—help.

WADE There's a kid, up there! I'm goin' in.

SECOND FIREMAN Come back. Come back, Wade. You fool— you can't make it— The crazy fool.

LITTLE GIRL [SOBBING] My mother's in there.

SECOND FIREMAN Stand back—stand back, everyone—the wall's gonna crash any minute.

VOICE Look out!

SOUND *Screams; Crash* (FADE)

COMMISSIONER You realize, Mr. Dawson, that six people burned to death in your building—five tenants and Fireman Wade.

DAWSON Yes, sir—but it wasn't my fault, Commissioner.

COMMISSIONER That's what I'm trying to find out. You say that the cellar was clear of all rubbish.

DAWSON Yes, sir.

COMMISSIONER One of your tenants, Anthony Abbatta, tells me a different story. He says your cellar was loaded with rubbish, Mr. Dawson—that the stairways were blocked with all sorts of boxes—that your fire escapes were shaky—

13

DAWSON [HURT] That's not true, Commissioner; why—one of your own inspectors was there earlier in the day.

COMMISSIONER Who was that?

DAWSON Dan Killefer.

COMMISSIONER Call in Mr. Killefer, please. *(FADE)*

COMMISSIONER You say, Mr. Killefer, that you investigated the building about noon of the day of the fire?

KILLEFER Yes, sir.

COMMISSIONER Was it a thorough investigation?

KILLEFER Yes, sir—a thorough investigation.

COMMISSIONER And you saw no irregularities at all?

KILLEFER No, sir.

COMMISSIONER That will be all, Mr. Killefer. *(FADE)*

COMMISSIONER [RESIGNED] Gentlemen, under the circumstances there is but one verdict we can return: *Fire—due to causes unknown.* *(FADE)*

SOUND *Slow, heavy footsteps—on creaky stairs. Cough. Door opens.*

MINNIE Hello, Harry.

BERGER [FATIGUED] Hello, Minnie. [COUGHS]

MINNIE [ANXIOUSLY] I see you still got the cough – pretty bad?

BERGER Just a cold – hangs on.

MINNIE Maybe you ought to see a doctor. You have it more than a month now.

14

BERGER What can a doctor do – I ask you—a pill he'll give me – a slap on the back and that's all. [COUGHS]

MINNIE Come – I got supper ready. Sammy's in the bedroom studying. I'll call him.

[HARRY IS SEIZED WITH A VIOLENT FIT OF COUGHING]

SAMMY [COMING ON] What's the matter, Pop? [FIT CONTINUES]

MINNIE Sammy. Run – get the doctor. *(FADE)*

DOCTOR All right, Mr. Berger—once more if you please. Breathe in. [BERGER COUGHS VIOLENTLY] Okay. You can button your shirt now.

MINNIE Doctor—what is it?

DOCTOR Oh—May I see you in the kitchen, Mrs. Berger? Just relax, Mr. Berger—and take it easy.

BERGER [FADING] Thanks, doctor, I will.

MINNIE Tell me, doctor—what is it?

DOCTOR Mrs. Berger—I'm awfully sorry—I've bad news for you.

MINNIE Please, doctor.

DOCTOR Now, take it easy. Getting excited won't help. Your husband has tuberculosis.

MINNIE [SUPPRESSES SCREAM]

DOCTOR Mrs. Berger, your husband's got to get out of this place immediately.

MINNIE Where?

DOCTOR The sanitarium. If he stays here, he'll be dead in six months.

MINNIE   How long has he had it, doctor?

DOCTOR   Oh, it's hard to tell. How long have you been living here?

MINNIE   Four years.

DOCTOR   That's about when it started. This place caused it. No wonder——no light, no air, no sanitation—not even a window in the bedroom. I'd advise you and your boy to clear out of here as soon as possible—or you'll get it, too.

SOUND   *Door opens*

[MINNIE SOBS UNRESTRAINEDLY]

SAMMY   Mom – don't worry. It'll be all right. I'll get a job.

MINNIE   No, you're going to school—you're going to finish.

SAMMY   But, Mom—

MINNIE   You heard what I said, Sammy. I'll take in a little work at home. Jacob's boss—he's sending out finishing—piecework —I can do it here.

HARRY   [OFF] Minnie.

MINNIE   Yes, Harry.

HARRY   Come here. [PAUSE] I heard what you said. [LAUGHING SADLY] Piecework! Is that what we came to Chicago for—you to do sweatshop work?

MINNIE   Harry – I got to – 'til you get better.

HARRY   [SADLY] 'Til I get better. Minnie, Minnie. You don't have to tell me what the doctor said—I know.

MINNIE   [TRYING TO JOSH HIM] King Solomon. What do you know?

16

HARRY I know.

MINNIE Harry – everything will be all right.

HARRY Sure – everything will be all right. [COUGHS] *(FADE)*

CARMELLA Ouch!

MARY Whatsa matter, Carmella?

CARMELLA Needle. This finishing job.

MARY Why hurry so fast?

CARMELLA I got a date with Angelo – gotta meet him at eight. It's ten to, now. That's why I took the stuff home to do—I'd never finish it at the shop—that dumb boss always hanging around.

ROMANO Why you no invite Angelo up here?

CARMELLA [LAUGHS MIRTHLESSLY] Invite him up here? In this filthy hole—Papa, I'm ashamed to. There—that's that.

SOUND *Breaking thread*

CARMELLA I'm going to change into my new flower dress, now. [PAUSE] Uh,– Papa – will you please face the wall? – I'm going to change.

ROMANO Sure – sure – I turn around – I no look.

CARMELLA You too, Salvatore.

SALVATORE Aw right, aw right—who wantsa look—who do ya tink ya are – Cleopatra?

ROMANO Salvatore – don' be so smart. [PAUSE]

CARMELLA All right. You can turn around now. How do you like it?

17

ROMANO Thatsa fine lookin', Carmella. You're very pretty girl – like calendar picture.

CARMELLA Thanks, Pop. Well, – I'm going. Good-bye, Papa. Relax, Mom.

MARY Have a good time, Carmella.

ROMANO Yah – enjoy yourself.

SOUND *Door opens*

CARMELLA Thanks – I will. So long.

SOUND *Door closes* [PAUSE]

SALVATORE Well—guess I'll take a walk myself.

ROMANO Where you going?

SALVATORE Get some fresh air—you know, *fresh* air.

ROMANO What about your lesson?

SALVATORE I can't study here. You oughta know that by this time.

MARY Don' go to the poolroom—— they're bad – bums.

SALVATORE Listen, don' call my friends bums. They're nice fellas. Well—don' take any wooden nickels.

SOUND *Door opens and slams*

MARY Joseph, I'm worry about Salvatore.

ROMANO I know, Mary, this dirty place.

MARY [SIGHS] If we could move to nice place—clean, – light. Carmella not ashamed to bring friends up. Salvatore meet nice boys.

ROMANO [MONOTONE] This dirty place—dirty place. *(FADE)*

SOUND *Footsteps on sidewalk*

SALVATORE Hello, Dipper. H'ya, Phil.

DIPPER H'ya kid.

SALVATORE Whatya guys gonna do tonight for excitement?

PHIL I dunno. Whataya say we walk up Grand—you know—near the saloons.

SALVATORE Not a bad idea.

DIPPER Yeh – some of dose old gaffers around there – all hopped up.

PHIL Yeh – wit' a lotta loose change on 'em.

SALVATORE [SLIGHTLY FRIGHTENED] You mean—we'll jackroll 'em?

DIPPER Whataya tink we're talkin' about—tiddledewinks? Whatsa matter—scared?

SALVATORE No – no – I ain't scared. Come on. *(FADE)*

SOUND *Weak, irritable crying of baby; Cradle squeaks*

SOPHIE [SINGING SOFTLY] Rock-a-bye, Baby, on the tree top, When the wind blows, the cradle will rock—

[BABY CRYS LOUDER]

SOPHIE [ANXIOUSLY] Baby, baby—what is it?

MRS. KLEPAK Don' worry, Sophie. Baby be all right—just tired.

SOPHIE I don't know what to do. He won't eat anything—just cries the same way all day long.

19

MRS. KLEPAK Don't worry—he be better. Sophie, I'm taking soup to Mrs. Barolla downstairs. She very sick – fever. When Stanley comes in, tell him to wait—I be right back.

SOPHIE All right, Catherine.

SOUND *Door opens and closes*

SOPHIE [RESUMES SINGING] Rock-a-bye, Baby, on the tree top. [HUMS]

SOUND *Door opens*

SOPHIE Hello, Stanley. Your mother said for you—why, Stanley,— what's the matter?

STANLEY [VERY WEAKLY] I dunno—I don't feel good—I got a headache—head hurts—

SOUND *Thud of body striking floor*

SOPHIE [SCREAMS] Stanley! Stanley! [BABY'S CRIES MOUNT] (*FADE*)

VOICE I: [WHISPERS] Typhoid!

VOICE II: [DITTO] It's spreading!

VOICE III: [LIKEWISE] Contagious!

VOICE IV: [SAME] Unclean!

VOICE I: [ONCE MORE] Keep away! Keep away! (*FADE*)

COMMISSIONER Dr. Hamilton, what in your opinion was the *one*, *primary* cause of this epidemic?

DR. HAMILTON Mr. Commissioner, there was no *one* cause. Several factors were involved. Gross negligence on the part of the Authorities. Typhoid would *never* have become as widespread as it did were it not for the criminal carelessness of the city

20

inspectors – *or* their being open to arguments of favored landlords. There was also the matter of the wretched plumbing and sanitary appliances. There were the toilets, used by several families in common, being located in cold, dirty hallways. No, Mr. Commissioner, there was no *one* cause. I'd say the *combination* of *all* these factors was the *primary* cause of the epidemic—— in short, the existence of slums. *(FADE)*

VOICE III: [SLOW AND DELIBERATE] *What price slums?*

ANNOUNCER Rickets.

VOICE I [WOMAN]: Three out of every four babies in the slums has it.

ANNOUNCER Tuberculosis.

VOICE II [MAN]: Six times as prevalent in the slums as in other areas.

BERGER'S VOICE *(FILTER MIKE)* [COUGHS] Just a cold – it hangs on – what can a doctor do? – just a cold. [COUGHS]

ANNOUNCER: Financial Loss to City.

VOICE III [MAN]: In one year Chicago spent more than three million dollars to provide ordinary services such as police and fire protection for one square mile of slum area. The taxes amounted to little more than a million dollars. Since they were fifty percent delinquent, the actual ratio of income to outlay was one to five.

ANNOUNCER: Juvenile Delinquency.

VOICE IV [WOMAN]: More than twenty-five percent of the adolescent boys is slum areas passed through the Juvenile Court in one year.

SALVATORE'S VOICE *(FILTER MIKE)* Yuh mean jackroll 'im? No – No – I ain't scared—come on – come on.

ANNOUNCER: Typhoid.

VOICE II [MAN]: During the epidemic one thirty-sixth of the population suffered one-sixth of the deaths.

SOPHIE'S VOICE *(FILTER MIKE)* Baby – baby – what is it – what is it?

MUSIC *Fast – Mounts to crescendo*

SOUND *Crowd noises; Rapping of gavel, Noise subsides*

VOICE [CLEARS THROAT] —and do, gentlemen of the City Council, the new building codes just passed provide, among other things, that every building shall have adequate fire-escapes, windows in every room, water closets in each apartment, proper facilities for garbage disposal, and adequate ventilation. We believe that with the enforcement of these codes, the blighted area of Chicago will be eliminated. *(FADE)*

SOUND *Rattle of dishes*

ROMANO I tell you, Mary, everyt'ing be all right now.

MARY How you mean, Joseph?

ROMANO Alderman pass new law – make landlord fix up place nice. What they call it, Carmella?

CARMELLA [HAPPILY] Building codes, Papa. Things will be different now.

ROMANO [GAILY] I know all time everyt'ing gon' be okay. [LAUGHS] *(FADE)*.

DAWSON [ANGRILY] Now listen, Kramer, does it mean I have to fix all my places this way?

KRAMER It looks like it, Dawson.

DAWSON But I can't do that—it'll cost a fortune. I'm in this business for profit, not for love. What with taxes and all these new-fangled improvements, I won't make a cent out of my buildings.

KRAMER Now don't you worry, Dawson. Let me do the worrying—I'm your lawyer.

DAWSON Well, you better start figuring something out pretty quick—or I won't be needing a lawyer.

KRAMER [SLOWLY AND SLYLY] I think I see an out.

DAWSON You do? What?

KRAMER You know—I believe all your property can be exempted from the law.

DAWSON [EAGERLY] How's that?

KRAMER Did you ever hear of the Constitution? We're going to fight these codes on the grounds of their being ex post facto legislation.

DAWSON What's that?

KRAMER You'll find out. *(FADE)*

SOUND *Crowd noises; Pounding of gavel*

JUDGE [POMPOUS] It is the decision of this Court that these building codes constitute ex post facto legislation. That is to say, they cannot apply to buildings already in existence, but are applicable only to buildings not yet constructed. Otherwise, these codes would be unconstitutional in that they would involve unwarranted interference with the rights of private property. *(FADE)*

DAWSON [GLEEFULLY] We did it! We did it!

KRAMER [SMUGLY] I knew there was nothing to worry about. Of course, if you intend to build new houses, you'll have to conform to these laws.

DAWSON [LAUGHING] That's a hot one. I'm not interested in new houses—the old ones'll do just as well. After all, my tenants don't pay too much rent so they'll have to be satisfied with what they got. No, thank you, I'll keep my houses just the way they are. *(FADE)*

CARMELLA [BITTERLY] Just the way they are! That's the way we'll have to keep on living with things just the way they are.

ROMANO [CHILDLIKE – PUZZLED] I don't understand. What the judge mean—says law no help us?

CARMELLA Oh – I don't know. Something about the Constitution.

ROMANO I don't understand this.

CARMELLA I do, Pop. I'm beginning to, anyway.

ROMANO What you mean, Carmella?

CARMELLA Papa. We don't count – people like us don't count to people like Mr. Dawson. They don't care what happens to us. Some day – I don't know why – but I feel it – some day the *government's* going to do something about this. *(FADE)*

MILLER So you see, Westcott, that's the set-up. The Romanos, the Bergers, the Rodzinski's – millions like them—constitute our slum-dwellers. And you see now – it's not *their* fault.

WESTCOTT Yes – I can see that all right. I may have been a bit hasty in my judgment – but what's the answer to all this? I know the problem—what's the solution?

MILLER The answer? What Carmella Romano was driving at – that some day the government would do something about it.

WESTCOTT Oh – government housing, eh?

MILLER Exactly. With the profit motive eliminated, the government could provide low-cost housing for these forty million people.

WESTCOTT Now wait a minute, Miller. Suppose the government does build on a large scale – how do we know these people will keep their *new* homes clean and decent-looking. I'm still from Missouri.

MILLER That's a fair enough question. Suppose we look in at one of the new government housing projects – how about the Jane Addams Apartments on Roosevelt Road?

WESTCOTT Okay. *(FADE)*

SOUND *Knock on door. Door opens*

MRS. MATUSAK Why – Carmella. Hello — come in – come right in. It's about time you paid us a visit.

CARMELLA Hello, Mrs. Matusak.

SOUND *Door closes*

CARMELLA I passed by the place so I thought I'd drop in.

MRS. MATUSAK Come right in and make yourself at home.

CARMELLA [AWED] My – this room—it looks wonderful – so light and airy.

MRS. MATUSAK [PROUDLY] Come in the kitchen and take a look.

CARMELLA A refrigerator! How lovely! [SOFTLY] Mama always dreamed of a kitchen like this—that oven and that sink!

MRS. MATUSAK Here's the bedroom. Look—two windows.

CARMELLA I can't believe it! Are all the flats this way?

MRS. MATUSAK Of course.

CARMELLA You mean for a room like this you pay only seven dollars a month?

MRS. MATUSAK Seven dollars and thirty-eight. That's right. We pay twenty-three fifty a month for these three rooms – and no extra charge for gas and electric light.

CARMELLA You're very lucky, Mrs. Matusak. It must be wonderful to live in a home like this.

MRS. MATUSAK It is, Carmella. You remember how hard it was for us to get along on Halsted – with Tony's eighty-five dollars a month? Now we can make easy – because this place is so cheap and nice.

CARMELLA Mama would love this place—and I could just see Papa sitting near the window there—smoking his pipe.

MRS. MATUSAK I wish you could be with us.

CARMELLA So do I. [SUDDENLY] And you keep the place so neat.

MRS. MATUSAK Of course, it's easy. It's not like the old place— no matter how hard you tried – it was dirty. Here – everyone keeps her place looking nice. See – I brought these new curtains last week—and we're saving up for a little rug in the living room. Oh,– Carmella – when are you coming in? We have a social club here—with discussions and shows – recreation playgrounds for the children.

CARMELLA I wish we could move in here – but there isn't much of a chance, though. We filed our application months ago.

MRS. MATUSAK I know it's hard.

CARMELLA About one out of a thousand is taken in. They've got a waiting list a mile long. If only the government would build more houses, we'd have a chance. *(FADE)*

DAWSON   No sirree! I don't like to see the government putting its nose where it don't belong. [CONTEMPTUOUSLY] Building apartment houses! You know what that is—it's *socialism* – that's what it is!

KRAMER   Yes, Dawson – something ought to be done about it. It sounds unconstitutional in some way—an invasion of property rights.

CARMELLA *(FILTER MIKE)*   Property rights! Property rights! What about human rights? What about us? Why did Harry Berger die in a sanitarium? Why did the Rodzinski baby die of typhoid fever? Why did my brother, Salvatore, die in the electric chair? Listen—you men in Washington! We, too, are the people. We want homes—clean, decent homes to live in—with plenty of sunlight and fresh air—homes where we can live like self-respecting American citizens— we want homes we'll be proud to call our own.

MUSIC   *"Home, Sweet Home"*

Photographs

Andrew Ritchie

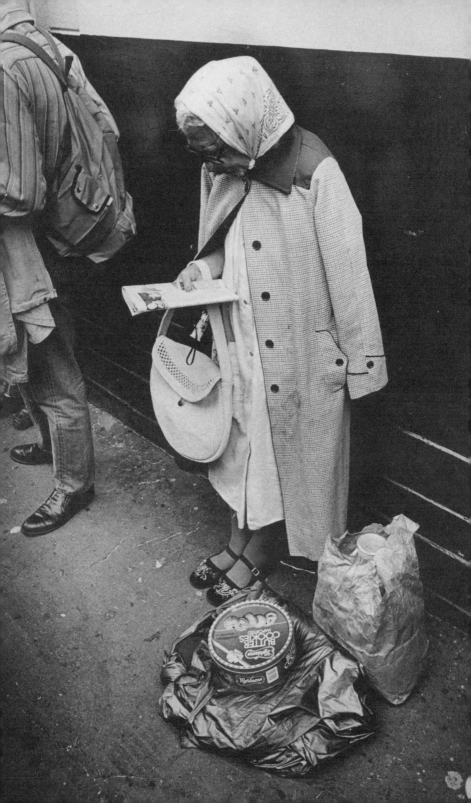

Tooth Fairy

Lisa K. Buchanan

Ella hobbled across the park to the fountain, pushed up her coat sleeve, and retrieved a few coins from the tile floor. The old woman drew her faded toothbrush from its plastic container and dutifully brushed her teeth. Afterward, she stretched her finger to the bottom of the container and pulled out a small piece of frayed, yellow newsprint: "Miss Ella Downey will become the cherished wife of Mr. Richard Burns, Saturday, April 1, 1944, Grace Chapel." She sat on the grass next to the cement path and placed her plastic bowl and Spare Change sign in front of her, gathered her army blanket from her hiding place in the bushes, and chugged down the last gulp of her sour wine. She tucked her dusty, orange bag beneath her, lay back on the grass and closed her eyes. The fierce wind whipped and distorted the faint voices of Grace Cathedral's Sunday evening choir from the other end of the park. The clock tower bonged into the night.

She felt a cold tap on her forehead and in a panic, flung her eyes wide open. A blur of patent leather shoes and fine boots walked along the cement pathway inches from her face.

A man's quarter hit her forehead and slid onto the grass in front of her nose. She pulled her army blanket around her, tucked her hands into her armpits, and fell back into the old days at the Fairmont with Richard. She sat next to him with three of his friends at a small, round table in the Venetian Room. The night had been wonderful; she had danced almost every dance with one or another of her husband's friends—businessmen in fine tailored suits, military men, colonels, admirals, sergeants in bold, starched uniforms with badges and medals. Richard didn't dance. There were countless bottles of champagne, and hairdressers, corsages, silk stockings, netted hats and low-cut gowns, brass horns, engraved cigarette cases, a drawer full of lipsticks, men pulling out chairs and twirling her around the dance floor. It was the jitterbug, the polka, and long dances, slow and sweet. They had taken limos everywhere, speeding around the city in fancy carriages behind darkened windows. Those were the good times when she and Richard lived at the Fairmont.

A tall man in uniform—trim, taut, and handsome—helped her into a big fancy carriage. "C'mon Cinderella, out of the cold," he said.

"But I'm so tired from dancing, my feet are aching," she pleaded. "Just let me sleep."

"C'mon Cinderella, where it's warm," he insisted gently. She pulled her shawl around her, tucked her bag securely under her arm, and took the coachman's gentle hand. He helped her up the steps and into the carriage.

"Cinderella never gives ya any trouble," the man said to the driver.

Ella woke up in a panic on a hard cot in a dim, shabby room full of other sleeping people. How did I get here, she wondered. What time is it? Where am I and who are these people? Where's my blanket, my spare change, my bag, my bag, where is my orange bag? She leaned over the edge and looked under the cot, relieved to find her bag sheltering her most valuable possessions: her pink toothbrush in its plastic container and a tattered copy of Cinderella.

Streams of dawn light crept through the cracks of thick, dark curtains and poked at her temples like knitting needles. She put her toothbrush in her mouth and chewed slowly as she curled up into a fetal position, her knees hanging over the edge of the narrow cot, her head throbbing. Ella reached into her pocket for toothpaste, but instead found a twenty-dollar bill. Must have been that tooth fairy, she sobbed gratefully. Now she would be able to buy a month's supply of toothpaste, and maybe a hat or some fancy shoes so that she would look nice when Richard arrived. In her head, she made a list of all the things she could buy with twenty dollars. She fell asleep, one hand clutching the crumpled bill, the other gently holding the ratty toothbrush to her lips.

The sun, bright and harsh, beat on the side of her face as she stepped down a noisy street, the damp wind threatening constantly to take her shawl and blind her with her own hair. It was an ongoing battle that day to keep her orange bag from sliding off her shoulder. After a few blocks, she recognized the busy one-way street in the

Tenderloin district. Angry drivers of the morning rush strained their vocal cords and picked fights over lane changes. Loud, crude men emerged from the girlie places and shouted obscene things at Ella.

"Yow, baby. Look at those legs," a barker yelled, then laughed obnoxiously.

"What kind of a bag lady are you? Just one bag to your name?"

"Yeah, maybe when you grow up you'll have a shopping cart," another one said.

Ella chewed her lips and shuffled along in silent terror. She clutched her crumpled twenty and trudged slowly up the steep hill toward the Fairmont, reminding herself with each step that the tooth fairy had finally come through, and that Richard must be on his way, and that as soon as she got to the top of this hill she could treat herself to a bottle of whiskey. Then she would go into the Fairmont and get gussied up for Richard. She would be home, where nothing bad ever happened.

When she reached the top of the hill, she heard the clock tower strike noon. A victory. Ella laughed aloud in the corner store, and laid her twenty dollars proudly on the counter.

"A fifth of Seagrams," she declared, "and this tube of toothpaste." The man put the whiskey and toothpaste in the bag, and Ella slipped the change into her coat pocket without looking. That was extravagance, not having to count the change, she mused.

At the fountain, she brushed dutifully till her gums hurt, and then some. She rambled across the park and sat on her favorite bench facing the entrance of the Fairmont. She opened her whiskey and took a mighty swig. A few people turned around to look at her. They must recognize her, Ella figured, as she watched fancy people come and go across the Fairmont's marble porch. She took long, luxurious swigs of sweet, warm liquid, content for the afternoon.

Eventually, the glamorous figures in front of the hotel doors fuzzed into the twilight. Dusk descended and blurred everything, everything but one man, tall and broad in a soldier's uniform. Ella watched him walk briskly across the marble porch and onto the street, looking intently at the ground in front of him and scratching his head. He was a handsome friend of Richard's who had come looking for her, walking toward her that very minute after she had waited so many years. Richard must be waiting inside with a big bouquet; the desk clerk must have told them she was in the park. Ella smoothed her hair with her

37

hands. How long had it been so dry and tangled, she wondered. She breathed deeply for composure; she didn't want to look too eager. As the soldier paused at the park entrance, scratching his head and scanning the area for her, Ella slipped her toothbrush from her bag and knelt down behind the bench, brushing ferociously, then rinsing with the final inch of whiskey. Extravagance, raving extravagance, she whispered, then stretched her finger into the toothbrush container to check her treasured, yellowed wedding announcement. For a moment she felt dizzy and sick, but she was not going to ruin the evening, her comeback to the Fairmont. She had waited so many years to come back.

She sat on the bench waiting, watching, showing off her creamy white shoulders in a long taffeta evening gown, delicate strings of diamonds gracing her neck, her ankle. She reached for her fur wrap and was shocked to find her dusty knitted shawl. The handsome man turned and looked at her for a long time. She saw him smile faintly behind the shadow of a streetlight. He walked quickly toward her, anxiously, nervously scratching one of his ribs, his broad shoulders and slim physique forming a silhouette that Ella planned never to forget.

But when he sat on the bench next to her, she felt a wave of nausea and disappointment. He was handsome, but he wasn't one of Richard's friends. Too young, too scraggly. He wore a faded combat uniform with a torn sleeve, one leg caked with dirt. Ella looked down at her own clothes and realized they were in the same condition. But she had that twenty dollars, and tomorrow she would buy a taffeta gown. She could practice her conversational charms on this handsome man tonight and be all dolled up for Richard.

"Want a cigarette?" he said, lighting one for himself.

"No. Thank you," she replied timidly and began to chew her lips. Coy and elusive. She had always been that way with her men at first. She gazed ahead at the Fairmont.

"What's your name?" he asked. She smiled shyly and looked again at the hotel. Maybe he would ask her to dance.

"In the mood, that's what he told me…" She sang the tune softly, carelessly, as she demurely refused his first request.

"Personally, I don't like to go tellin' people my name either." He paused. "But maybe when we know each other better." He scratched his ear nervously. "Normally I hang near the Panhandle. Guess we

38

both like parks." He scratched vigorously at a red patch on his collar-bone. "'Cept it gets kinda rough out there. But I've kicked a lot of ass in my day. When someone gripes me, let me tell you, I don't let 'em get nothin' on me. I can make a weapon out of anything...," he trailed off, scratching his shoulder and waiting for her response.

"You been hangin' here long?" he asked after a long silence.

"I'm waiting for my husband," she replied haughtily, looking straight ahead. A tall woman in a gold, silky evening gown climbed out of a taxi; the doorman lit her cigarette.

"Does he live in this park too?"

"No," she replied, laughing at the man's ridiculous question. "My husband is away on business right now, but when he returns we will live again in Room 637 at the Fairmont Hotel."

"That's a good one," the man laughed and slapped his own knee so hard that it made Ella flinch. He drew out a small bottle of generic whiskey, took a gulp, and passed it on to her. She refused. The lady in the evening gown danced on the marble porch with a man in a tux and back tails.

The man next to Ella continued to cackle, whiskey spraying out between his lips.

"Now wait just a minute," she protested playfully. "I'm truthin'." Ella furrowed her brow and pouted, then began to tell him about the old days. It was good practice for her comeback. She hadn't told anyone about Richard in years.

"Well," she started, "My husband and I met right there in the Venetian Room one night, back when I was a pretty thing, just eighteen. Well, actually, it all started before that. Ya see, actually, I'm— well you're not going to believe this but here, look at this." Ella removed the *Cinderella* book from her orange bag and opened it to the first page, the cinder-wench sitting by the chimney fire.

"Look familiar?" she asked, glowing.

"Yeah, when I was overseas we all used to sit around a fire too, except it was outside in the jungle and we were the watchmen and—"

"No, no, not the fire! Me, stupid! That's me in the picture! I was Cinderella!" Ella took the plain wrap whiskey from his hand and had a swig, smacked her lips. From the dazzled look on his face, she knew she had charmed him.

"Ya see, soldier, it's like the story, except this book has it all wrong in places. It's not a fairy godmother, it's the tooth fairy." Ella pealed off a loud cackle. The soldier laughed along with faked enthusiasm.

"See my picture here with the ugly stepsisters? They threw my ass all around the room whenever they felt like it." Ella made large throwing motions back and forth with both arms as she spoke. She turned pages sloppily and continued her story.

"Shhh. Hey, sweets, you're yellin' like a pig," he scolded. Ella composed herself.

"Anyway, then I met the tooth fairy, one night after this tooth right here fell out." She pulled back her lower lip and pointed to an empty space halfway back.

The soldier laughed, and Ella laughed along with him, spilling whiskey out of the bottle as she drank.

"And she told me to brush for an hour each day of my life and I would meet the most handsome and kind man in the world. You can imagine I started brushin' right away."

"So then," she continued, "one night I wore one of my stepsister's pretty dresses and took me out on the town. I came right here to the Venetian Room to hear the Andrew Sisters sing the apple tree song and that's where I met my Richard, my prince."

Ella paused and straightened her spine. "Richard Burns and I fell madly in love and got married the next day, April 1, 1944, right there in that little chapel next to the Grace Cathedral."

The street soldier took another draw from the bottle. "Did you say Richard Burns?"

"Yes, yes, that's my husband's name, that's my husband!" she said eagerly. "Richard Burns. Do you know him? He has lots of friends here in San Francisco." She waited anxiously for the soldier's reply.

"Nope, sorry. Sounds like a great guy though." Ella sank back into her shoulders for a moment, then sat up to speak.

"See, the book's all wrong. For one thing, I never forgave my damn stepmother." Ella was distracted for a moment by the woman in the evening gown who was kissing the man she had danced with on the marble porch. Ella sighed with longing.

"Anyway, we lived in Room 637. And we stayed out real late every night with his friends, dancing to Dorsey and Miller, Artie Shaw, Tex Beneke. And the men paid for everything," she boasted.

By then the street soldier had dozed off, leaning his head against the back of the bench. Ella continued her story, practicing for

Richard's return. "And ya know what else," she whispered to the snoring soldier, "all of Richard's friends adored me. Richard wasn't the jealous type. In fact, he was proud that I entertained his buddies— he said, long as I loved him, long as he was king. And he was a gentleman. That man respected me. That was back when I brushed my teeth all the time."

The soldier snored and Ella talked, no longer stumbling on her words. "And it was a lot of fun, but after a few months, I got tired. Richard always got mad when I said I was too tired to go dancing and he made me go anyway. Sometimes I put mascara on my eyelashes and I'd be so tired I'd cry and the mascara would come right off. I'd do my eyes five times in one night, then brush my teeth for an hour. I'd dance on my poor feet all night with Richard's friends. I was always exhausted and my gums were bleedin' from all that brushing and Richard got mad at me 'cause I wasn't keeping up and things got worse and it was just too much!" Ella began to sob. The soldier was still, except for occasionally scratching his neck in his sleep.

"And then, one day, Richard had gone out of town and I tried to get in the room, but it was locked and—"

Ella chewed on her lips and made herself stop crying. This kind of conversation would never suffice when Richard came back. She squeezed her eyes shut, breathed deeply, and continued to chew her lips until she pushed the locked door from her mind. She would be beautiful again tomorrow for Richard. Maybe they would even get their old room back with the soft, clean sheets and king-size bed, maid service, and orange juice in the morning.

Ella woke up on the bench the next day with the giant cathedral bell pounding the twelve strokes of noon into her ears. The left side of her rib cage ached; a bruise had swelled. She immediately checked her orange bag; her toothbrush and *Cinderella* lay undisturbed. The soldier was gone, along with her army blanket and toothpaste. She checked her coat pocket, no money. How was she supposed to fix her hair or buy a new dress for Richard's return? Two empty bottles lay on the grass beneath the bench. Ella tipped each one to her lips just to make sure. She put her toothbrush in her mouth, wrapped her arms around her head and curled up again on the bench, with Richard Burns caressing her shoulder and kissing her neck softly as she slept.

41

Kristen Wetterhahn

He be Santa

Maxine Hong Kingston

One Christmas in a big city where it snowed, maybe New York or Chicago, Wittman and his father were walking through a train station. A man in a ragged coat moved away from the pole he was leaning against. His hand came out of a pocket and brought out a toy, a plastic horse. "Say thank you," said Ba. "Say Merry Christmas." The three of them shook hands Merry Christmas all around. Wittman held the toy horse and watched the man walk out of the station. His father said, "He's Santa Claus. That was Santa Claus." Then they were in an elevator with an old man, who kept looking at Wittman. As all of them were getting off, the old man gave him a little green car. His father said, "That's another Santa Claus. He be Santa Claus too." And out on the street, a lone man reached inside his coat and gave him a stocking bag of candy. Many Santa Clauses. Santa Claus is a bum-show, and he does not have a sack full of toys. These men's pockets were not bulging with more presents for other boys and girls. They didn't have a family or a home; they had had enough money for one toy, and they'd gone out into the city to celebrate Christmas by choosing one boy to give the gift to. And because of his haircut and clothes or his Chinese father, they had chosen him.

Teen-age time, he stopped going places with his father, out of shame. He ought to give him a thrill and make the rounds with him one of these days. Appreciate a father who doesn't dictate much, nor hit, drink, nor hang around having habits that use up all the room.

Januaries, they had gone to American banks and stores to collect calendars of the solar year, and Februaries, to Chinese banks and stores to collect calendars of the moon year. On the pages of time: Guan Goony, god of gamblers, beautiful Hong Kong girls, fairy girls who float among birds and bats and flowers, kids riding on deer. The world is full of free stuff. The 365-page calendar. The food in back of supermarkets. His father hoisted him into the garbage bins, where he handed out cheese in plastic, cereal in boxes that the grocer had slit opening the shipping carton, day-old bread, pies in tinfoil pans. Bread gets a week old at home anyway before you get to the end of the loaf, right? At the state legislature, probably in every state, you can get all the scratch paper you want—the bills that didn't pass, and the ones that did pass and were acted on already, stapled together into legal-size notebooks, print on one side only—tossed out by the mound in the basement. A day out with Pop was filled with presents. The world was a generous place.

Another outing, he and Pop had gotten themselves invited to some kind of a club, and in the men's room, they filled their pockets with combs, razor blades, tiny tubes of toothpaste. It hadn't been that fancy a club, no valet. Pop hadn't lifted the silver shoe horn, but the two of them had taken off their shoes and horned them back on. Wittman, playing rich man, had left a check for a trillion godzillion dollars.

When he went to live in Berkeley, his father showed up and took him to the back of India Imports. They recovered enough stuff to decorate his room—a madras bedspread with a stripe that hadn't taken the dye. Pop got a poncho, and Wittman a sweater from Brazil, a strand had unraveled. A few of the earrings he took for hanging in the window. Never buy a bed, you can always take in a mattress from off the street. Find it before it rains. His school desk was a card table, one of many he'd found by the curb. Must be gamblers throw them out if they get unlucky. Eat in cafeterias where the condiments are on the outside of the cash register. You buy a serving of rice or some bread, and then you load up with relish, onions, salad dressing, Worcestershire sauce, ketchup. Never leave a restaurant without taking the packs of sugar and jam. (In that same *Oracle* wherein Mescalito looks like Zeppelin, Gary Snyder says for gleaners to come to the docks. The forklifts poke holes in sacks, and you can scoop fifteen or twenty-five pounds of rice once a week.) (Grocers are padlocking their bins shut.)

How to break the news to a wife that she's married a Cheap Chang? Don't worry; she's going to be supported in a way that isn't going to sacrifice his free life. And she's going to have to help out. He'll teach her how to live on nothing, and she'll always be able to get along, with or without him. For her birthday and anniversary, take her out to the dining rooms that feed any old body, such as the Salvation Army and the Baptist mission. Not the Saint Mary's kitchen, though, because of pride, too near the Chinese. Don't go to the Red Cross, either; after battles they meet soldiers carrying back their dead, and charge them for coffee and donuts. For Wittman's twenty-first birthday his father took him to a Skid Row blood bank, and they gave blood for ten dollars apiece. The Red Cross and the blood bank don't preach. Father and son, self-made men out of dregs and slag.

—from *Tripmaster Monkey – His Fake Book*
by Maxine Hong Kingston

Kristen Wetterhahn

In Memory of Lou Lou

Pat Andrus

Lou Ellen Couch, 22, known to her friends as Lou
Lou, was stabbed to death last Thursday night. "She
died the way she lived, defending a girl more vulnerable than herself."

—*Seattle Times*, December 1985

Lou Lou died today
and the press was courteous to note her passing
they even mentioned she protected street kids
herself out there eight years

Lou Lou died today
and my 14-year-old lives
a daughter who ran those same streets
one whom Lou Lou might have sheltered
one like many, scared and alone
when licensed predators appeared
poisoning the night with sweet talk

Lou Lou died today
and my daughter will arrive home by six
eat a full meal, sleep in her quilted bed
and Lou Lou's bed will be cold
and Lou Lou's street children
if they're lucky
might find dry earth under viaducts
a wine-soaked blanket
a scrap of cold pizza

Lou Lou died today
and her children, our children
burn with survival energy
for they too have visions
a possibility in their dreams
but they too fear earth's destruction
attempt escaping the mushroom cloud
crave needles and pills
grieve in their alcoholic haze

Lou Lou died today
and the people at the funeral
stand crying in small circles
try remembering some ancient land
where roses grew free and wild
where music was played at dawn
where children lived out their dreams

A Home of Her Own

John Grey

All she ever wanted
was four walls,
a roof over her head,
lights, food,
and somewhere warm to sleep.

She now has this.
The entranceways to
the Crick Building
and Fortescue Apartments
comprise a total of six walls,
though she doesn't complain
about the extra two.
Each has an awning above.
Street lights glare into
her makeshift alcove
looking for fugitive shadows.
The dumpster parks a block away,
always a few leftovers
in its darker reaches.
And her own arms wrap round her
through the bitter night
like the memory of a caring man.

Bag Lady

Kathy M. White

gypsy strong, armpits
of fox and bay leaf,
fingers through worn gloves,
eyes, puffy marshmallow.

her lips, dried elm leaf,
she drops an overcoat to the floor,
empty rags of the melted
witch of the west.
morning stench in the first-floor
bathroom of city hall.

in the park, children run and tease
her umbrella going through autumn
sycamore leaves, her shoes, haiku
of basho, journeying through the streets,
pockets of salt, old postage stamps,
matches, violets, green butterflies,
crickets.

how long since she slept in white night
gowns, left the bathroom, waterfall thin
and clean, whirled a child under laurels?

Ripening by Degrees

Bill Cowee

Like early western homesteaders,
Mary squatted on a plastic
green grass landscape island
at the corner Arco station,

hazel eyes darting to possessions
walled off by rows of baling twine
spun between dwarf palm trees
whose shadows swept seductively

along the ridges of her sagging face.
Light tripped on the frayed, exhausted
beach chair where Mary Theresa nested
except for the early call of morning

when she flung back her angora hair
and hefted a corrugated apple box
under a slack and trembling arm
for the trip to market, to market.

Sharp-eyed produce clerks culled them.
Cauliflower gone checkerboard black,
fist-size cabbage peeled to white leaves,
a puckered tomato caving in on itself,

two hairy oranges, grey-green and leaking,
gold-teared black bananas crying to be bread,
loose grapes that never dry to raisins
in the damp corner of the dumpster.

She was in her own heaven, bent over
rummaging in that cold green steel box,
sorting scattered succulents at her feet.
Now, climb the side, over the edge of plenty,

over the cat who screeches and leaps,
over the refuse discarded in heaps
go home now, before the fading shadows
are trimmed, culled by the rising light.

Commuters slow, pause at the gas station
staring, whispering to the car pool
as Mary breakfasts...occasionally looking up
to wave a greeting with a limp celery heart.

Northern Dreams

Gordon DeMarco

It was hot. Almost seventy degrees and it wasn't even eight A.M. yet. Maybe not a scorcher by the yardstick used by folks in Detroit or Chicago. There they only begin to talk about the heat when the tar seams in the street pavement begin to bubble, or when old men who have forever been seen only in yards and yards of baggy gabardine roll their pants up to their knees, exposing pitiful, lumpy pink legs.

But for San Francisco it was hot enough. The brown hills were bleached to an irritable, flammable straw, and the earth was as dry and lifeless as an insurance policy. And if you know San Francisco, you know that few buildings have air conditioning, and shade trees are just now beginning to catch on. So there is little relief for the citizenry when the temperature climbs into the nineties as it had done for the past three days.

True, one could go to the beach for refreshment, but when you were pushing sixty-five, like Rudy Giggins was, and you looked like one of those geezers from Chicago or Detroit with your pant legs rolled up to the knees exposing a pair of legs that would send little children running to their mothers, it was out of the question. Besides, Rudy didn't like the ocean. "Too noisy," he would say, if anyone asked, though no one ever did. But that's what he would say. "Too noisy and too smelly. I got an allergy to seaweed, too. Makes me sneeze something fierce." Yes, he had it all figured out what he'd say if some smart aleck came up to him and said, "Hey old-timer, you look pretty hot in all that gabardine. Why don't you go to the beach and cool off?"

But even on a day like this it wasn't likely anyone would say such a thing to him. In fact, it was unlikely that anyone would talk to him at all, except maybe order him to move on. He liked sitting on porch steps and watching the cars and people go up and down Cortland Avenue. No, ever since Lenny died in the spring there hadn't been anyone for Rudy to talk to. He and Lenny had been pals for more than fifty years. Probably closer to sixty. They grew up together in the shadow of the Firestone Tire & Rubber Company in Akron, Ohio. Lived on the same block, were in the same class in grade school, played on the same baseball team in the summer, graduated from high school together, and went to work in the tire factory the very same day. Both Rudy and Lenny worked swing shift at Firestone—plant no. 2—in the bead room, before the war broke out. Then they went down and signed up together and spent eight weeks in the same platoon at boot camp before being shipped overseas.

They were both sent to Europe, but served in different outfits and in different campaigns. It was the first time since they were small boys they had been separated. They didn't see each other for nearly three years. Then, one day in San Francisco, both fresh off different troopships, they ran into each other in a bar on Powell Street. It was a joyous reunion for them and they made a pact right there at the bar to never leave San Francisco and to become partners for the remainder of life's journey.

"That was nineteen forty-six," Rudy said, reminiscing out loud. "We had us some great plans then." He paused to look across the street. A young woman was pushing a baby stroller up the hill. He remembered when she was pregnant. It seemed like it was only a few weeks ago, but the baby in the stroller looked to be at least two years old.

It was only eight o'clock in the morning, but Rudy felt like a wheel of soft cheese under all those clothes. *If it gets much hotter*, he thought to himself, *I'll have to take off my jacket.*

Rudy spit on the sidewalk and watched his saliva evaporate in less than a minute. He sat on the porch steps with his elbows on his knees and his head in his hands. He wished there was someone he could talk to. Talk to about Lenny and him and the times they had. But who would want to listen to him, "an old stumblebum livin' in the past," as he described himself on more than one occasion.

"Yeah, we had us some pretty good times," he sighed into his knees. But the good times ended more than seven years ago when Lenny got sick. He had some kind of lung disease that grew slowly but progressively worse until it killed him. "It was that powdery stuff they was loadin' down at the warehouse," Rudy always said, "That's what got 'im."

Five years ago Rudy moved in with Lenny to take care of him. They each had their own room and there was a small living room, but the quarters were cramped. That's why Rudy was out on the street so often. "Gotta get away from that snotty old lady once't in awhile and get me some fresh air," he would say jokingly to Jake, the man who ran the grocery store at the end of their block.

Rudy and Lenny fought a lot during those five years. Fought about things most people fight about. For Rudy, it was an agonizing time. He knew Lenny was dying, but he wanted desperately for him to recover so they could go on one final adventure together. They had talked about going to Alaska and the Yukon to pan for gold ever since they were kids and listened to "Sergeant Preston of the Yukon" on the radio.

"You gotta quit playin' sick," Rudy would say, half in jest, to the bed-bound Lenny. "If you don't want to go to Alaska, just say so. I'll go by myself."

"Just restin' up a bit so's I can scoot up them mountains," Lenny would always reply. "I know I'll have to be carryin' the likes of you on my back most of the way up."

"Don't you wish. I'll get to the top of ol' McKinley and I won't even be outa breath. You just watch."

"I'm not callin' you no liar, Rudy, but I seen you run outta gas between the grocery store an' here, an' that's only half a block up a dinky little slope."

"There's just no talkin' to you. You been in bed so long, you turned into an old fogey. Your piss is backed up into your bloodstream. That's why you're so ornery. No other way to explain it."

"Well, what's your excuse? Why're you so cranky all the time?"

And so it went for five years until that day last spring when Lenny ceased being an old fogey, forever.

The heat depressed Rudy. Thinking about Lenny depressed him. And being in San Francisco depressed him. "What was it the fellow called it?" Rudy used to say to Lenny. "Baghdad-by-the-Bay? Ha! More like Palookaville-by-the-Pacific if you ask me."

It was always followed by a complaint session on what they didn't like about their adopted home. "Too many hills; not enough shade trees like we have back in Ohio; the he-shes are takin' over the town; the buses are always breakin' down, and car drivers are maniacs; the cops are too damn mean; everything's set up for fancy lawyers and computer programmers; no good restaurants where you can get meat-loaf and mashed potatoes, and you can forget corn on the cob." Sometimes they would spend a good part of the day running down the city in which they had spent nearly their entire adult lives.

"She's a beautiful lady," Rudy would say, "but she's changed on the inside. They took away her soul." Lenny would nod in agreement. If he wasn't having one of his coughing fits, he would throw in his two cents' worth. It was one of the few things they agreed on.

"Yeah," Rudy would say, "Frisco's been pretty good to us. But things is changed. Time to move on to greener pastures." That's when he would go to the closet in the hall and get the maps of Alaska and the Yukon and the travel brochures and bring them into Lenny's room and spread them on his bed.

"Yessir," Rudy would say, going over their imaginary itinerary for the thousandth time. "We'll take the ferry from Seattle to Skagway. Get us some gear in Skag and hit the Chilkoot Trail to Bennett Lake. Then we can pack on to Whitehorse or take the White Pass train. Which do you think we should do, Lenny?" It was a question asked a hundred times.

"Oh, I don't know," Lenny would say. "Depends on how we feel." It was an answer a hundred times given.

But now there was no one to share the dream. And no money to make it happen. And besides, Rudy didn't want to go by himself. He never did anything without Lenny. Not until five months ago. Now, most of his time was taken up with mourning the loss of his friend and their dream. That was something he did all by himself. It was almost the only thing he did. Except drink, that is.

Maybe if he didn't drink so much and saved his money he could take a little trip somewhere. Maybe Lake Tahoe. But there was little money to be saved. The rent ate up most of the small Social Security check he received each month. In fact, if his financial situation didn't improve soon, he would have to give up the apartment. And he knew the only place to go from there was a Tenderloin or Mission district transient hotel. But there was no way his situation could improve. He hadn't worked since before Lenny got sick and now he was too old to do much of anything that would produce an income.

It was getting on to nine o'clock. Rudy stood up and took off his jacket. He thought about what he would do for the rest of the day. That was the hard part—the planning, the thinking about what to do. Most days he would go home and watch television or take a bus downtown to the Strand Theatre and pass the day with a triple feature. Recently, the movies had been getting better. It made the days more tolerable.

Rudy reached into his pocket for his wallet. If he were to go to the movies he would have to audit his financial situation. He opened his billfold. A five-dollar bill and two singles lay inside. He squeezed them between his fingers to make sure of the count. Once he thought he had only two dollars in his wallet, but when he checked it again he found a twenty-dollar bill sandwiched between the two ones. Ever since that time he always counted the bills twice, running his fingers over them in the hope that a shy twenty was hiding next to a bill of lesser denomination.

But no such luck this time. Seven dollars, that was all. There would be no more for three days, until his Social Security check arrived in the mail. Three days on seven dollars and thirty-five cents. It was one more thing to dampen Rudy's already soaked spirits. A pack of smokes, another dollar less to spend. That would leave him with a little over four dollars for food. A dollar thirty-three a day. Maybe a little more since there was a can of soup and a relatively new box of Hi-Ho crackers back at the apartment. Maybe that tuna salad in the refrigerator was still good. He would have to check when he got home.

Rudy hitched up his pants and threw his jacket over his shoulder and started up the street. He stopped at Jake's grocery store for some cigarettes.

"Hey, Old-timer," Jake said smiling. It wasn't a friendly smile, but neither was it sarcastic. "Haven't seen you for a while. Thought maybe you finally made it to Alaska."

Rudy looked at the small television behind the counter that Jake ran continuously during store hours. Rudy wasn't interested in the program. It was just somewhere other than Jake to direct his eyes. "Still workin' on it," he said to Jake. "But I'll get there, all right. Don't you worry none about that."

"Sure you will," said Jake with a chuckle. "What can I do for you in the meantime?"

"Gimme a pack of Chesterfields, willya Jake?" Even Rudy's brand of cigarettes were from a bygone era.

He walked out of the grocery store and up the small hill to the apartment. He wanted to drop off his jacket and maybe take a look in

57

the closet to see if he still had that short-sleeved shirt he bought at Penny's so many years ago. He figured the heat wouldn't let up until nightfall and a short-sleeved shirt would be mighty welcome until then.

It was still hard for Rudy every time he walked into the apartment. Even after all these months. Lenny's stuff was still there. The place was kind of like a mausoleum without the body and it made Rudy feel funny.

He picked up the mail and walked inside. He put the three envelopes and the flyer from a discount drugstore on the kitchen table and went to his room to look for the short-sleeved shirt. Fifteen minutes of digging through a chest of drawers and two cardboard boxes full of clothes that might have hung on the racks of a Salvation Army Thrift Store a dozen years ago, produced a blue shirt with large white flowers printed on it. He took off the shirt he was wearing and put on the short-sleeved shirt. Instantly he felt cooler.

He walked through the kitchen on his way to the front door. He stopped to get a glass of water from the tap. He took the glass to the table and sat down. "The heat slows a man down," he thought to himself, "and he must conserve his energy whenever he gets the chance."

Rudy sat quietly sipping the water and looking at the wall above the table. Or rather, the picture on the wall, a picture of him and Lenny at boot camp before they were shipped overseas. He reached up to pull it down. "No need to have that old thing starin' me in the face all the time," he growled. But his hand stopped before it reached the yellowing photograph. "Ah, hell – might pull some of the paint off the wall. Better leave it 'til I can figure out a way to save the wall. Don't want the landlord to slap any extra charges on me for destroyin' his damn property."

He casually fingered the morning mail as he stared wistfully at the picture. He flipped through the pages of the mailer from the discount drugstore without enthusiasm. A second piece of mail was an offer from cable television. The third was an envelope with a return address from somebody he had never heard of. Some kind of insurance company. "Somebody sellin' somethin' else I don't need," he sighed as he opened it and read the contents.

"*Dear Mr. Giggins:*

"*Mr. Leonard Fazzio, recently deceased, was an insured policy-holder with our firm. As you are named in Mr. Fazzio's policy as sole beneficiary,* *you are entitled to survivor's benefits. Please find enclosed a check for the amount of $1,837.00 as your full entitlement.*

"*Very tru—*"

"Eighteen hundred and thirty-seven dollars," Rudy repeated softly, almost reverently, like an Ave Maria. Then "eighteen hundred and thirty-seven dollars!" like an old football yell, followed by "eighteen hundred and thirty-seven dollars!" like an incantation from the basso profundo in a Wagnerian opera.

Rudy got up from the table and looked at the picture of him and Lenny. His hand shot out and ripped it down. He held it in front of him. Tears rolled down his leathery face and onto the blue shirt with white flowers.

"Lenny," he said out loud. "Lenny, Lenny, Lenny! You sly old devil. You never told me you had an insurance policy." He turned abruptly and ran from the kitchen to the hall closet to get the maps of Alaska and the travel brochures. He waded through the thirty years of papers, books, mementos, and receipts, all the effluvia a person collects during a lifetime. "Oh, to hell with it!" he said after a brief and unsuccessful search. "I know how to get there in my sleep." Once again he looked at the photograph, still in his hands. "Thanks, old buddy," he said. Then he lightly kissed the picture and placed it face down in one of the boxes of his important papers.

Rudy threw some clothes in his old brown, striped suitcase. Five minutes later he was out the front door and on the street. He never even bothered to look back and check to see if he had locked the door, a routine he went through every time he left the apartment. He went straight to the corner on Cortland Street where he caught a bus to Mission Street. There he cashed the insurance check at the check-cashing service located next to the unemployment office.

A half-hour after that, he was at one of those used car lots on South Van Ness that sold automobiles of questionable quality at bargain prices. He peeled off five one-hundred-dollar bills and gave them to one of the lot salesmen in return for a 1968 Buick which he immediately christened "The Spirit of Lenny."

It was maybe ten-thirty or eleven in the morning. The car radio said the temperature was 87 degrees. Rudy was on the Golden Gate Bridge.

Father's Afterlife

Bernice Rendrick

I think of my father:
Is he in hell? at home again?
a pitchfork prodding him,
his life spent there
on the fire—
brain burnt like a red hot
socket, twisted wires fizzled,
spurts of yellow tobacco juice
dribbling from his mouth
and a trembling coffee cup
to slurp at bitterly
during his best times.

My mind tracks him
along Kansas highways or railways
as he jumps from a boxcar,
weaves into a gloomy roadside bar,
thumbs on to Barnum and Bailey's,
flips breakfast flapjacks,
tugs up the big tent
and roasts in the comfort
of freaks and sad clowns.

And then back to the hospital.
Always back to the hospital.

I think of him
as if even at this impossible
distance between life and death
I must track him still,
find in the cinders
of his afterlife
a shard to warm
my own cold twisted hands.

Laddie's Tears

Michael Daley

I left Portland on nothing but a breeze.
The train moved up Columbia Gorge,
a late moony light
spreading over my cheek,
flashing on the splinter floor.
My hands were cold stones
banging the pockets of a big green coat.
I saw his white beard float
over fields tilled by moon,
heard him talk all night,
weary as prayer, mirroring his life
on the fields of corn, mustard, alfalfa.
In the moon a girl raised her hand
to her long hair.
We were close to the garden.
She waved her baby's hand to us
standing in the boxcar door,
and a rapid pulse
flew along my throat.
When I woke at dawn
he was whispering. *All day*
a jug under the peach orchards.

I found him singing in the Market,
little Polish tunes with a cup out
as shoppers passed us,
small dried flowers, purple & white,
blowing out of his pockets.
1931, the first night
in the pit of a boxcar,
Milwaukee already sleeping
inside his father's pasture,
he cried for those knit
pillow cases stuffed

with feathers of a goose he plucked.
There is a ship, he tells me,
travels across space
playing Louis Armstrong. Fifty years
on a golden record.
I want to be there,
his fingers curve over the air,
but where is space? where is it?
The moon can bear a footprint
for a hundred windless years.
He squeezes his fists,
smoothes the ground under peach trees
to offer wine he's tasted forty years,
and tenderly
pours his cup of quarters
into my pocket.

Baby It's Cold Outside

Rajat Neogy

"Baby," of course, is a rolled-up overcoat or backpack, your pillow for the night. The cold is everywhere. San Francisco is one cold city when it's cold.

I was lucky for a couple of weeks; a friend had left the cab of his pickup truck unlocked for me to use when it got dark.

Five weeks of searching for a room in the North Mission district was fruitless. There were no vacancies in the numerous hotels; rooms were customarily contracted out to the city's "housing program," a far more lucrative and assured way of a guaranteed income on a two-day basis than from the elusive transients' weekly rate.

So, hotels with up to a third of their rooms unoccupied claimed NO VACANCIES, in stark, crudely lettered signs or complacently blurted-out mispronouncements of the English language.

Eventually, the nights got too cold, even in the pickup cab. And then the rains came—dripping methodically, slipping through the cracks of the windshield and doors, misting up the inside with a secondary dampness that no amount of stuffed newspapers could absorb and no amount of blankets could ward off. Like an invisible fog, the frosty chill settled into the bones.

Numbed desperation goaded me to ring a friend for advice, someone who had connections to the city's emergency shelter programs. Like anyone roughing it in the Mission, I was aware of their existence but not of how to use them.

I was lucky. She made a number of phone calls, and in about ten minutes she gave me the name and address of a hotel where I could register after work (at nine o'clock that evening) and stay for two nights. It was the...

MIRADI HOTEL on Hyde Street.

After checking in with what would become a familiar stern stricture—

"No guests or visitors/Check-Out 8:00 A.M./Leave your
key at front desk on your way out"

—I took the elevator to the fifth floor.

A whiff of curry told me at once that the owners and management were vegetarian East Indians. Although my foot—and heart—sank in the lush red carpeting of this "posh," touristy-looking hotel's lobby, I was anxious to see what my room offered.

When I accustomed myself to the light, I could not believe my eyes! Two large single beds, an attached bathroom complete with shower and toilet, ample closet space, and a color TV!

After bathing and slipping between the clean white sheets of the comfortable bed, stretched out my full length for the first time in centuries, it was obvious to me that heaven couldn't hold more blissful delights.

The two nights were over much too soon.

The hotel had been provided by the Housing Hotline, but for my next accommodations I would have to do my own footwork. This procedure is worth noting for its eccentricities. It involves the following: (1) Finding your way to 150 Otis Street, arriving precisely at some time between 9:00 and 11:30 A.M. (which depends on the frame of mind of the official you hear it from), and being given a ticket—a number. (2) Then, whether or not you've picked up a number, you are told to come back at 1:30 P.M. This is important to remember: They do not give you one unless you know to ask for it. (3) You return at 1:30 whereupon you are asked if you have a number. If not, you must stand in line for one. If you have one, you join about sixty to a hundred people already seated on stackable plastic chairs. (4) Starting around 2:30, monotonic numbers are called out. If you're lucky, yours is one of them; if not, you're asked to return the next day. There are only so many rooms and hotels to be assigned. (5) It's now about 3:30. But you are lucky—your number is called. You are given a "voucher" with the name and address of a hotel, which is good for two nights. (6) You're to check in at the hotel after 5:00 P.M. but not later than 6:00 P.M. if you want the room, regardless of your work schedule. (7) You register at the hotel (which could be anywhere from the Tenderloin to South of Market or the

Mission) and try to return to your night shift. (8) You wake up early the second morning, check out, and back to the address above in (1) for your next shelter hunt.

If you apply for a hotel on a Friday morning, depending on your good fortune and the official's discretion, you may be assigned a room for the weekend (i.e., three nights) and then return to practice the same on Monday. Thus, so as not to be homeless on Sunday, it is worthwhile to skip Monday and start the process over on Tuesday instead.

On the average, you will spend over six hours to get a roof over your head for thirty-eight hours, which you will actually use for sixteen hours at best. An expensive ratio of 3:8 in time, energy, and stress, not to mention uncertainty.

My next hotel was the...

ANXIOUS ARMS on Folsom and Sixth.

I misread the name as "Ancient Arms" but no, it *was* Anxious. I wondered what comforting arms might embrace me.

This, too, turned out to be a pleasant experience in spite of the seedy address. The hotel was clean and neat with a kind of rustic homeyness and thoughtful little touches like sealed water glasses on the sink, soap and fresh towels, and little wrought-iron tables—even one in the bathroom with an ashtray. Pleasantly civilized and restful.

My stay here ended on the Friday morning after Thanksgiving Day. There were no rooms for the weekend, Friday being a state holiday as well. By and by, I wound up at the...

EL CAPITAN, at Mission near Twentieth.

This hotel had acquired a notorious reputation over the years and is generally regarded as "the jailhouse" by knowledgeable locals.

Entering through steel-barred doors substantiates it, as you are suspiciously buzzed in. This elaborate security does not extend to the privacy of your room. Room number 209, which faces the street, was noisy and dilapidated. Shards of a broken mirror dislocated my face as I stared at it over a sink where only one faucet worked; the mottled bedside rug was askew.

On the second night, I entered my room, where my backpack and other belongings were clearly visible on the side table, to find a complete stranger asleep on my bed. Summoning the manager brought apologetic explanations and an improvised bed somewhere in a corridor where I lost my bearings and my glasses in the early morning chill.

The toilets were unusable and without paper. You begin to feel a stranger to yourself as you lay in bed. I left early and returned shortly after noon to my backpack, handed over to me by a female desk clerk without so much as a glance.

No sign of my glasses.

(On the sixteenth of December, under the headline "Welfare Mom's Plea for Decent Housing," a newspaper article recounted the Dickensian conditions the mother and her daughter lived in and the systematic harassment she suffered from the manager. It came as no surprise to me that the squalor described was found at the El Capitan.)

After two or three more turndowns at the Shelter Hotline (no vacancies as Christmas drew nearer), I called my friend again for help. In any case, I was tiring of these perpetual two-day relocations. This time my resourceful lady friend put me in touch with the shelter at the Salvation Army, where the maximum stay was two weeks.

SALVATION ARMY SHELTER, Eddy Street.

I quote from their intake leaflet, which speaks for itself: "Hours of Operation, 6:00 P.M. to 6:00 A.M. daily. Gate Opens 6:00 P.M. (You sit in an open yard until…) Admission Begins 8:30 P.M."

You are let in four at a time; you undress, shower, stash your clothes and belongings in garbage bags, and change into the pajamas they provide. Coffee and sandwiches served at 10:00 P.M. Wake up at 5:00 A.M. Dress, stand out in the dark courtyard for coffee and donuts. Wait until 6:00 A.M. to leave.

It is difficult and unsafe to do much in the Tenderloin at six o'clock on a winter morning, except watch the street sweepers or the garbage trucks.

Salvation Army Shelter rules are simple: No alcohol or drugs; no smoking or eating in the building; no weapons; no violence or threats; no disruptive behavior. Disregarding any of the rules results in instant dismissal.

The fourteen-day stay must be used consecutively, after which you have a ninety-day waiting period before being eligible again. Children need not apply. (Most runaways know they'd probably just get turned in to the same Foster Care authorities they're running away from.)

Salvation was truly Army in style.

In a longer account, I could detail the conversations exchanged and the people met in this "off-street brotherhood" (unspoken familiarity and simple coexistence on the pavement as initiation). One can admire the patience and stillness of so many different individuals who have to erase time between the inevitable lines, the hours between one door opening after another is shut.

It is an endless kaleidoscope of perpetual immobility. A very un-American, non-American activity.

Five days later at midday, I was walking around Sixteenth Street, paying off bills. It was dark when I woke up to bright lights and green-masked figures peering down at me.

I was told I was in the intensive care unit in San Francisco General Hospital, being treated for hypothermia. I was covered with hot lines everywhere: oxygen in my mouth, penicillin in my arms, several IVs wherever a vein showed.

I was told my body temperature had been down to sixty-five degrees Fahrenheit.

These hot lines were shelter, were life. San Francisco General was warm.

Photographs

Alan Harris Stein

The Chicago Union of the Homeless in action

Oral History

Otis Thomas

I first found out about the union when I was layin' around a Center for Street People, and the organizing team came out and passed some flyers for homeless people to get involved, to change the quality of their lives, to go beyond shelters, to form a union. And when I read the piece of material that was put before me, I thought that this was something that I wanted to get involved in because number one, this was the only thing out there to give homeless people an opportunity to explain, or tell, or change, or fix what happens to them. I was laid off, I used to work, and it took me a good eight to nine months to admit that I was homeless. When I joined the union, a week later we had our founding convention. At our founding convention we had 250 homeless people. We had people from the Church, people from the *union* union, unions to support our efforts, so we had all kinds of people there, outside of homeless people. So we elected a president, a vice-president, and a secretary-treasurer. From there, a couple of months later I seemed to be a little bit more advanced in bringing out the knowledge of homeless people so I was sent by the (National Homeless) Union to a school which is called the Committee For Dignity and Fairness, in Philadelphia. And that's where the first Homeless Union started. And they were so much more advanced than us that they saw the need to have a school to take homeless people, to educate homeless people to some of the things and why people are homeless. I thought that, you know, I really thought there were some people on the street, that they were out there 'cause they really wanted to (be there). When I went to the Institute, I stayed there seven weeks dealing with the problems of homelessness, homeless people, shelters, politicians, the whole scope of reality—facts! So when I came back here I was able to use the knowledge that I acquired in Philadelphia. We continued to protest, we continued to pull more people into the union, we continued to get out into the street and organize other homeless people, because, there again, a person that hurts can't explain to anyone *how* they feel. I cannot explain to you about a broken arm, if I don't have one. So we are, we're organized and still are organizing homeless people to come into the union.

Home

Jack Hirschman

(to the National Union of the Homeless)

Winter has come.
In doorways, in alleys, at the top
of church steps,
under cardboard, under rag-blankets
or, if lucky, in plastic sacks,
after another day of humiliation,
sleeping,
freezing,
isolated, divided, penniless,
jobless, wheezing, dirty
skin wrapped around cold bones,
that's us, that's us in the USA,
hard concrete, cold pillow,
where fire? where drink?
damned stiffs in a drawer
soon if, and who cares?
shudders so familiar to us,
shivers so intimate,
our hands finally closed in clench
after another day panhandling, tongues
hanging out;
dogs ate more today, are curled
at the feet of beds, can belch, fart,
have hospitals they can be taken to,
they'll come out of houses and sniff
us dead one day,
pieces of shit lying scattered here
in an American city
renowned for its food and culture.

The concrete is our sweat hardened,
the bridge our vampirized blood;
the downtown, Tenderloin, and Broadway
        lights—our corpuscles transformed
        into ads;
our pulse-beat the sound *tengtengendeng*
of coins piling up on counters, in
phonebooths, BART machines, *tengtengendeng*
in parking meters, pinball contraptions,
public lavatories, toll booths;
our skin converted into dollar bills,
plastic cards, banknotes, lampshades
for executive offices, newspapers,
        toiletpaper;
our heart—the bloody organ the State
gobbles like a geek in a sideshow
that's become a national circus of the damned.

O murderous system of munitions and inhuman rights
that has plundered our pockets and dignity,
O enterprise of crime that calls us criminals,
terrorism that cries we are fearful,
greed that evicts us from the places we ourselves
        have built,
miserable warmongery that sentences us to misery
        and public exposure as public nuisances to
        keep a filthy republic clean—
this time we shall not be disappeared
        in inner-city ghetto barrio or morgue,
this time our numbers are growing into battalions
        of united cries:
We want the empty offices collecting dust!
We want the movie houses from midnight 'til dawn!
We want the churches opened 24 gods a day!
We built them. They're ours. We want them!

No more doorways, garbage-pail alleys,
no more automobile graveyards,
underground sewer slums.
We want public housing!
No more rat-pit tubing, burnt-out rubble-caves,
no more rain-soaked dirt in the mouth,
empty dumpster nightmares of avalanches of trash
        and broken bricks,
screams of women hallucinating at Muni entrance
        gates,
no more kids with death-rattling teeth under
        discarded tarp.
We want public housing!
we the veterans of your insane wars,
workers battered into jobless oblivion,
the factory young: fingers crushed into handout
        on Chumpchange St.,
the factory old: spat-out phlegm from the sick
        corporate chest of Profits.
Instead of raped respect, jobs
with enough to live on!
Instead of exile and eviction in this,
our home, our land,
Homeland once and for all
for one and all
and not just this one-legged cry
on a crutch on a rainy sidewalk.

Hunger Streets

Elly Simmons

On the Streets

Steve Abbott

I saw him walking up Haight Street, dragging an aluminum cart with a large backpack tied on it. He wore a dingy navy jacket with brass buttons. His black hair was chopped short and his face looked weathered, old beyond his years. He stared straight ahead. A *Sentinel* lay on top of his backpack, the commemorative issue on the Washington March.

Some of these guys were pretty once. They came to San Francisco from Alaska, Alabama, or some small Midwestern town. When they walked into a bar, men offered to buy them drinks. Their eyes sparkled then. Handsome guys wanted them, older guys offered jobs. Some promised love, others offered drugs that felt like heaven. You move in with somebody who says they love you. Where do you go when they kick you out?

"I can't imagine—if I was going to stay alive at all, that is—falling so low that I didn't have a place to live. I guess you must have so abused all your friends that..."

My student Chris has difficulty writing about the homeless. He can only describe certain street crazies, those whose pants are barely pinned on. When you live in the street, you take a street name: Tonto, Wildman, Little Brother. When you live in the street you join another society. "Look at this bracelet I'm makin', man. I don't like panhandlin'. Fuck, I'm no beggar. I make these bracelets and sell them on the street."

Not all the homeless live on the street. Some squat in abandoned buildings. Some are young, attractive, or charming enough to crash with people they meet.

"Lonely guys like to help you get your trip together," Spooky says. This cocky knight has so many colorful scarves tied around his legs that one wonders if he ever takes off his jeans. He has "the look," as Prince would say. He refuses to be invisible. A hope of intimacy, companionship, a hint of danger and excitement—that's the bait.

Rescuers and waifs come together like bread and jam, an almost magnetic attraction. Until, that is, the rescuer wants some nurturing himself. If statistics on the homeless included all those staying with "friends," the number of those listed as homeless in urban areas would more than double.

> To be born in the street means to wander all your life, to be free. It means accident and incident, drama, movement. It means, above all, dream. A harmony of irrelevant facts which gives to your wandering a metaphysical certitude. In the street you learn what human beings really are; otherwise, or afterwards, you invent them. What is not in the open street is false, derived, that is to say, literature. Nothing of what is called "adventure" ever approaches the flavor of the street. It doesn't matter whether you fly to the Pole, whether you sit on the floor of the ocean with a pad in your hand, or whether, like Kurtz, you sail up the river and go mad. No matter how exciting, how intolerable the situation, there are always exits, always ameliorations, comforts, compensations....

That's Henry Miller. He wrote *Black Spring* in France, 1934–35, when he was still young. But Henry Miller didn't know the army of young men who flocked to San Francisco, the gay mecca, in the seventies. Some settled into good jobs. Others just partied, hustled, fell by the wayside. How many remember Coca Vega for whom every day was Halloween? He made a brief splash in bars, in cafes, even in a movie. Then denial took its toll.

It's hard to glamorize crashing on speed and sleeping in dumpsters. It's hard to glamorize the life of a sixteen-year-old runaway selling his ass on Polk because McDonald's doesn't pay a living wage. It's hard to glamorize the life of a man with AIDS who can no longer work or pay rent. There's no exhilarating freedom in living on the street if you're sick, no drama if it's cold and rainy.

"You tell us to get off the street and go to the park," a street person tells a cop. "The cops in the park tell us to come here. So whada we supposed to do, man?"

Many became homeless when state mental institutions shut down, when businesses went bankrupt. An increasing number are young. I've heard of ten to twelve people sharing a flat, or even a studio. Our gay youth don't need more Boy Parties. They need decent paying jobs and affordable housing. And what of our gay oldsters? Will San Francisco ever open a gay and lesbian senior citizen center?

"My friend's real sick," Clint tells me. "She went to work anyway and now she's so sick she can't get out of bed. She has no medical insurance and her folks won't help her either."

"Why not get something together with her friends?" I reply. "Bring food, read poems, play music. Ask everyone to donate five dollars or whatever they can. We have to start learning to take care of ourselves."

But my suggestion's just a stopgap measure. Clint himself is homeless, has been staying with various friends for the past several weeks. With what he earns behind a coffeeshop counter, he can't afford more than two hundred dollars a month rent. Rents like that are hard to find.

"In Tokyo you can rent a plywood box for five dollars a night," Chris says. "It's just big enough for a sleeping mat. Each box has a TV, too."

Will San Francisco parks start filling up with plywood boxes, converted drainage pipes? If America's trade and budget deficits push the economy into a tailspin, will New York and San Francisco become like Rome, Mexico City, and Third World capitals where the homeless gather at the edges of the metropolis in shantytowns?

After World War II, when thousands of Germans were bombed out of their homes, Theodore Adorno wrote a brief essay on the homeless. If you own a home, Adorno said, all your physical and psychic energy goes into maintaining it. You imprison yourself. But if you rent, you have no stability or security. You're at the mercy of landlords and real estate speculators (the most evil of capitalists, according to Karl Marx and Walt Whitman). So what is one to do?

Some problems have no easy solution. You can only survive by choosing the lesser of evils. Or in Adorno's ringing conclusion: "Wrong life cannot be lived rightly."

untitled

Dennis Conkin

Head resting
on bony hands,
bent knees
nestled in
the half-light
where doorway
meets sidewalk,

the old woman
is asleep
beside an
empty shopping
cart, parked at
an angle
to the street.

Do not disturb her.
She is dreaming
of America.

World Apparent

Lisa Bernstein

She walked neutrally through the city
carrying a plastic bag from the drugstore.
Her calves and ankles were dirty,
nicked. She scowled at the well dressed
and the derelict, trying to hold the trembling inside her
motionless, like honey inside a comb
—it spilled into the muscles of her haunches.
She crouched next to a vacant lot
shaking down to her heels.

"Christ's thorns! How excessive,"
she scoffed. "Is that what suffering is, an old movie on TV?"
The people kept walking like wind-up toys
and her brain was a ring upon ring of burst berries
and she could mash them just by wincing
if she wished to, and swallow the juice.

Then she was Athena
mute and upright in the gutter,
sipping from a paper cup.
She was certain of something
but she couldn't name it,
the wafery taste in the air and water,
spongy, empty,
the victorious gaze of
what-was-it-called?
Forgiveness,
remembrance,

justice,
mind.

How did this fit
with the porousness of the
concrete buildings, the steel piles encased within them
visible, already rusted, the faces passing
so quickly but still she saw each pore

and the businessman's gleaming brow
over his bright, honeycomb brain
and then a girl with a transparent groin,
black chain wound around her ova—

She stood trembling on the sidewalk.
The crowd parted around her.

His Love

Sharon Doubiago

All morning the blue policemen
gather on the steps of the cathedral.
A line of children, Chinese, ribbon the park.
I read your poem to me, Human Love.

"A policeman's father died. Not
fifty. Heart
attack."

The hearse arrives. The widow,
her red bouffant above the mourners,
jerks up the steps. There must be
a hundred cars in the procession, red lights
spinning above the police phalanx.

The coffin is pulled from the back.
Here in the park we all turn to witness
how loved is the burden the bearers
stoop beneath. Climb. Now old men
escort young women up the steps. Brothers
daughters. The bell tolls.
Nine gold crosses

on the steepled spires
herald the city I hadn't realized
is of your old faith, *the spine*

of the dark man of your poem
hanging there, an editorial
on the limits of my love.
At my feet the white painted outline
of a murdered man.

I've been sitting outside your old church
two weeks now with the other homeless, we
inheritors resurrected from history.
I keep seeing you, my Love

in our tavern furthest north,
your forlorn head broken to your heart,
touching me. The holes
in your hands open and open
as you ask me to leave. How terrible
is our task
to get free of his spine, the Father

torn apart in the child. The cop.
The dead god in us unrisen.

As an Angel Glimpsed by Blake

Carol Tarlen

Standing near the doorway of a steel-
encased building, the man
in the worn, black suit
wipes soil from his frayed,
white starched cuffs and waits
for his son to enter, eyes lowered,
as the man, too, lowers his eyes.
This is the best he has,
the poverty he wears, his empty hands
a gift of shame for a son
who looks away.

I see the old man
in a darkened theater,
an image superimposed on scenes
of a filmed revolution,
slipping between shadows that fall
on slogan-plastered walls.
He is my vision, my DNA chain;
I circle my wrists with his hunger
that shimmers beneath my skin
translucent like a beached jellyfish
on oil-slicked sand.

Juana Alicia

On Your Way Home

Bill Clark-James

Someone kicks you in the side, and you wake up face down on the wet grass. You want it to be just a dream. But it's not a dream, and the toe in your ribs doesn't go away, so you roll over and look. Right into the eye of the sun. Close your eyes and see the bright afterimage burned inside your eyelids and hear the ocean.

"Hey, man," a voice comes from the afterimage, "give me some money. I'll go get some wine. I'm cold."

Cold, yes, cold, you agree, and open your eyes—slowly this time —and look at him. His face is familiar, but you don't really remember him.

You put your hands in your pockets, but they're empty. Leave your hands in them because they are warmer there.

"I don't have any money," you say.

"Well, where is it?"

"I don't know." What's going on here? Do you have some money? "It must be at home. I've got to get home."

You say this, and it sounds right. You had better get home.

"Not again, Willie. You did this last week." The face looks disgusted and leaves. Who's Willie? There's no one else around, so he must mean you. You want to ask him, but he's gone.

You sit up, look around, and realize the sound you thought was the ocean is really the traffic on the streets around you. The sun shines on your face, fighting a losing battle against the autumn chill. You hug yourself and feel your clothes. The dew soaked them while you slept.

Wait a minute, why are you sleeping in the park?

You don't have an answer, but think, again, *I've got to get home*.

Rub your face, try to stimulate the brain, and you feel the stubble of a week's growth of beard.

I don't have a beard, you think. What happened?

Try to remember, but you can't. Things are seriously confusing, not as they're supposed to be.

"I've got to get home." That much you know.

Stand up, and you find that a mistake. An intense rush of pressure swells your head, like a balloon being blown up. Your vision blurs, you see the world through cotton candy and feel like you just stepped off the Tilt-a-Whirl. All around you there is singing. Look for angels in the trees, but find only a few dead leaves and the sun, caught in the branches like Absalom. Absalom? Who the hell was he? You don't know. Maybe you had a cat named Absalom once.

A radio snarls from the open window of a passing car and replaces the angel songs. After a minute, the world seems more stable, and you try to figure out where you are.

Look for landmarks. Nothing tells you where you are, though everything looks familiar. Wander over to a bus stop and look at the schedule for clues. Maybe you could tell from that where you are, but you can't read the words. They might as well be Bulgarian, or Chinese.

You could read, memories tell you, and the words look English, but you don't understand them. The harder you stare, the less sense they make, until they look like ants dancing on the sign.

Maybe you're in a foreign county. Panic, and search the buildings for signs of reassurance. Through the trees you see an American flag in front of a golden-domed building across the street.

Start across the street towards the flag, but jump back at an angry scream from a car. You stumble and fall on the sidewalk. The people waiting for the bus step back and turn away, like you're some sort of diseased animal. Except for one small child. Beneath her curly blond hair, she smiles and giggles. You giggle, too.

The sound of singing rises behind you. Turn around and look for the angels again, but the songs come from a small group of people and make no sense.

Slowly, you get to your feet and read the schedule again. The ants have stopped dancing and you can make out some of the words, but still they're meaningless and still you don't know where you are.

There's a building to the south. How do you know it's south? You don't care; it's a point of reference. Follow the traffic toward it. As you approach the street you shake with fear, and shake more as you cross. When you reach the other side, you're trembling with excitement. Now the world is more in focus and things are becoming clearer.

Over the door on the east side of the building are the words: "The Public Library 1955." Think a moment. You know what those words mean.

This is a library. They have books here. Find the right book and it will tell you how to get home. But this isn't 1955. What year is it? You were thirteen in 1955, but you're not thirteen now. You're... You're older. How much older? When were you that young?

Suddenly, you're hit by a memory so vivid that it seems more reality than recollection, like seeing someone else, even though it's you.

At thirteen years old, his father gave him a shotgun for his birthday. They hunted ducks together. The flat gray sky mirrored the flat gray landscape. His feet were wet and cold. The small boat they crouched in stank of fish and whiskey. They waited all day in that skiff, but no ducks came.

You shiver with that remembered cold.

Someone's radio shatters that distant landscape. You walk as steadily as you can toward the doors and go in.

Stares greet you when you walk into the lobby: a leper in paradise. You'd better do something about your appearance. Head down the stairs to the bathroom in the basement.

Hey, wait a minute. How do you know there's a bathroom down there? You remember you've been here before. Many times, in fact. It's a warm feeling knowing. Your head is clearer and the world more defined.

"Is that really me?"

"Well, it's sure as hell not anyone else," comes a voice from behind you. You turn around and see that the doors have been taken off the stalls. A man sits on the toilet, pants around his ankles.

"Do you know me?"

He grunts, whether in disgust or with effort you can't tell, but doesn't answer. You look back to the mirror.

The face looks much older than it ought to. You're not that old, and you thought you had more hair than that. The face is oddly out of balance; one side sags. Grimace and find the muscles of one side are loose, almost flaccid. One eyelid looks at half-mast. Shadows beneath both eyes tell of late nights and too little sleep. The stubble of your beard reminds you of a cornfield after harvest, waiting to be plowed under. The buzzing light gives your skin a sickly green-gold look, like rotting hay. You have to do something about this.

Turn on the water and wash your hands in the sink. Water dark with grime comes off and gurgles sickly down the drain. After several scrubbings with harsh powdered soap, they look clean and almost fresh. You cup them together under the running water and fill them, then splash your face. The cold water stings. Splash again and rub your face, removing the dirt. After cleaning your face, you attempt to rinse some of the grease and filth from your hair. You decide that will have to wait for shampoo and a hot shower.

When you run your fingers through your hair, you feel a bald spot and a ridge of hardened flesh behind your right ear. Now, turn sideways and see in the mirror a faded pink half-moon of scar.

What happened here, you wonder, but don't remember.

"Is that where they took your brains out?" asks the man who had been on the toilet. When you look at him, he turns around and walks away without your answer.

Search your pockets and find two items stuck in the lining of your jacket: a wallet and a plastic pill bottle.

In the wallet there are three soiled and crumpled bills and a driver's license. Look at the face on the license and in the mirror; it's the same face. The name reads "Willard John Atwood," and there's an Albuquerque address.

Albuquerque? That's right. Home is in Albuquerque. But this isn't Albuquerque. This is somewhere else. Where? What am I doing here?

Look again in the mirror, and then down at the license. Those hands, you remember, worked with skill and precision on a drafting board. They held scales and templates, pencils and erasers, with a gentle touch, dirty with lead. Now, they are pink with scrubbing, and older. You flex them and they feel stiff. They shake with age and for the craving of alcohol.

Splash your face again, dry it on the soiled towel, and get out of there. That's better. Don't want to face that face too much longer right now. In the hall you hear children singing. Listen, you know this song. It feels much better now, as you start up the stairs, humming to yourself, "e-i, e-i, o."

When you reach the top of the stairs, though, you become dizzy and disoriented again. Sit on the steps for a minute until it passes. Uncertain of too many things, you walk across the lobby toward some couches and chairs beneath the windows that look out on the park.

"A book," you say aloud. "I'm supposed to be reading a book in the library. They won't see me if I read a book." You are afraid of stares.

You grab a book off a shelf and sit on one of the couches. The vinyl wheezes under you with a satisfied sound. You turn the book over in your hands and open it up. Once again, the words make no sense and float on the pages. Quickly, you shut the book and cry silently, so they won't stare at you.

"What's happened to the words?" you say, looking at the book. There is a yellow and orange sticker on the book's spine: an atom pierced by a rocket.

A rocket, you think. That's what I need, a rocket to take me home. I could get home if I had a rocket. I used to make rockets, didn't I? Maybe that's how I got here, on a rocket. I've got to get home. Countdown. Three, two, one, blast-off! Blast home? Blastoma. That's it. No.

"No," you say. You don't want those memories; but even as you say it, you remember—your vision narrows and fades into a white light.

In memory, the white light becomes the white ceiling of a hospital corridor, in which your remembered self waits. Watch as they wheel him into an operating room. He's not quite awake, but can see lights and masked faces. He sees them fade out as he sinks into sleep. Remember struggling out of dark unconsciousness into bright confusion. Finally the memories distill into a doctor standing by his bed.

"Mr. Atwood," he says, "we were able to remove almost all of the tumor. However, it was malignant and we cannot guarantee that it will not return. We appear to have affected some of your memories and capacities, but with drugs and rehabilitation, you should be able to live a full life again. Perhaps even a long and healthy one."

But after the operation, days and nights of pain continue.

Frustrated, unable to work, you begin to drink. Then, one day you leave your home. You don't know why anymore, but you leave.

❖   ❖   ❖

For a second time, you wake with the sun in your eyes. This time it's afternoon sunlight. You fell asleep with the book in your lap. You open it up again and look down at the letters on the page. It's like looking through a mist, though; nothing is in focus.

Where are you?

You don't know. You had known where you were, but now you have no idea. All you know is that you have to get home. You can't recall exactly where, but it's south of here. The thing to do is head south until you remember.

Stand up and your head feels that familiar rush. You're dizzy and hear angels singing again. After swaying in place for a moment, you're steady enough to walk, so you head toward the door.

At the gate, a furious beeping and locked bar stop you. Look around, and a man in a blue coat comes toward you.

"Sir, you need to have that book checked out. If you'll come with me."

Bewildered, you follow him. "I'm sorry," you say. "Sometimes I forget things. They made a hole in my head and everything fell out. I'm on my way home." You hand him the book and walk away.

Outside, the afternoon wind has begun to blow. Its fingers pluck your clothes, finding every hole, and cold air pours over you. You shiver.

Look around and see the bus stop. It looks safe, familiar, and you walk toward it.

The bus can take me home, you think. I'll just get on a bus going south. I'll be okay when I get home, it's warmer there. Why didn't I go home sooner?

Wind and sorrow bring tears to your eyes. You blink, and your watery vision makes gems of the streetlights just coming on. The world looks washed clean and radiant. You get to the bus stop just as a bus pulls up. Follow the line of commuters on, and walk past the driver.

"Hey," she says, "It's seventy cents. You've got to pay."

Stare at her. "I left my money at home. I've got to get home." You sit down.

"Either pay or get off, but do it now or I'll call the cops."

But you don't listen to her words; the light and warmth surround you with the womb's luxury, and you smile at the driver. This is what you wanted. Your body tingles as you sit there, and you smile wider. Shortly, though, two police officers, a man and a woman, board the bus and escort you off.

"Okay, what's your name?" the man asks.

The words growl around in your head, and the wind pounds like surf in your ears. You want to speak but can't move your mouth. Suddenly, your legs disappear, and you fall to the sidewalk.

"Drunk," the policeman mutters to his partner.

"Doesn't smell like it," she says, and searches your pockets. "What's this? Drugs?" She holds up the pill bottle and passes it to her partner. You wonder why they're not looking for your legs.

"Decadron," he reads. "Prescribed to Willard J. Atwood. Is that you?"

But you're not listening. You stare in terror at the black serpent coiled around the officer's waist. It's ready to strike at any moment.

"It checks with his wallet," the woman says. "New Mexico driver's license, expired last year."

"Hell, this prescription's two years old." He shakes the bottle and you hear the snake rattle. "Only been half used, it looks like."

"Let's get him in the car and over to Denver General, there may be something wrong with him."

They try to get you to stand up, forgetting you have no legs. You try to tell them that, but succeed only in making gurgling noises. After the second attempt you collapse on the sidewalk, trying to tell them your arms have fallen off too, but they don't pay any attention.

"This doesn't look good. Call an ambulance."

As her partner goes back to the car, she kneels beside you. "We're sending for an ambulance, Mr. Atwood. They'll take you to the hospital. You're going to be all right."

"Take me home," you say, but only the word "home" escapes.

"What?"

"Home," you repeat.

A gust of wind blows several strands of her hair across her face. Caught by the last light of the sun they glow like gold. She pulls them aside and tucks them behind her ear, smiling.

Suddenly, all the angels sing again, and as she stands up, her dark

97

The Prism

Richard Silberg

The prism is hanging in the window   where you left it
        I think of you   when I see the sunlight shattered in its colors

        I can't make it cohere   make the crippled facts come whole

the way I took you in at your eviction   tried to nurse you
        give you space   make you whole

Each spectrum is a vibrant ghost   white light broken into all the colors
ghost of science   of the ideal world   each spectrum is a droll creature
        a proof   like when I saw my own bones
        on the screen of Dr. Chomski's fluoroscope

Your house is still not rented   the neat blue trim childcare house
with the swingsets folded in the backyard
                the landlord putters 'round there at night

        I've tried to write about you, Ann   another fall
someone else going down   the rotting food   the dead goldfish
        in the whispering scraps of paper   of their lives

about watching the familiarity of your face   its purpose   its humor

becoming a hollow face

echoing

in which a murderer stalks its victim

I saw the devil there

I saw the headlight of a train hooting down a tunnel

this sunlight in my room is like childhood   each droll little spectrum

all the colors

an ideal world   a laughing god

What am I writing about?   I love you

Am I writing about myself?   always in love with the morning star

"sweet   sweet   you show me the stars in heaven"

There's an ache in my chest   the basket of my bones

a baby curled up and hating

the light of its passing shines through   an x-ray

Writing about writing?

How are you?   Will you be well?

I love you

a laughing god

the bones of sunlight   burning   to burn

the book of itself

life   this hot pained wandering

Yesterday's Byline

David Volpendesta

Pamela's ears were so attuned to the squeaks of the pulleys and the whirling noises of the motor that she could determine from their pitch at which floor the elevator would stop whenever she heard its doors open and close. Had she been directing a film—and the psychotropic drugs they had been injecting her with for the last two weeks glossed everything with the illusionary sheen of cinema—Pamela would have opened it in silence with a close-up of the flesh-colored elevator doors. Then the camera would focus on the panel of green numbers above the elevator, then the partition separating the elevator doors from the steel door to the stairway. Then, as the sound track came on, it would zoom in on the silver lock mounted on the wall opposite the partition, which summoned the elevator to the sixth floor of Saint Helena's. Finally, the mechanical eye would fall on her slippers and move up the hem of her dress until it came to rest on her thin face, gray eyes, and disheveled, blonde hair.

In her mind's camera Pamela had already blocked and rehearsed the next scene at least two dozen times. In a cubical office with white walls, she is seated in a black reclining leather chair in front of a Formica-topped desk. Behind the desk, sitting in a wooden chair, her right hand fiddling with a pencil and her left moving elegantly through her short, lightly moussed black hair, is Dr. Anne Thorton, the resident assigned to be Pamela's therapist.

"Pamela, you've been here for two weeks and you haven't told us anything except your name," the doctor states flatly in her New York accent. "We can't help you if you don't tell us anything about yourself."

"*We?*" Pamela reflects in a barely audible voice. "Why do you use *we* when you're speaking for yourself? I only see one of you. How many are there?"

"I was referring to the hospital staff."

"There was no antecedent to indicate that."

"I'm not here to argue semantics. You knew what I was talking about."

"Had I, I wouldn't have tried to clarify the pronoun for which there was no antecedent. I'm not here to teach semantics."

"The context was clear."

"The subtext was interesting."

As the camera begins to move away, Dr. Thorton drops her pencil on the yellow legal pad where she's been writing and looks at Pamela. Her eyes move slowly around the room until they lock onto Pamela's eyes, which in turn are fixed in the middle of the doctor's forehead.

"Look, Pamela," Dr. Thorton resumes officiously, "I don't want to send you to the state hospital at Napa, but you're leaving me no choice."

"No choice? You've already made the decision. Yesterday I saw my medical chart lying on top of the desk at the nursing station. I read the section where you'd written, and I quote, 'Patient's uncooperative comportment coupled with her psychotic symptoms make it expedient that she be admitted to the state hospital at Napa.'"

The close-up of Dr. Thorton's face captures the two white hairs in her widow's peak, records the stunned expression on her lips, and is perfectly still as she jerks in her chair, indecisive as to whether or not she should exert her authority. The jittery motion of her hands and her twitching lips underline her fear that she's losing control of the situation. Pamela sits back in the chair with her arms folded, her eyes moving from the pearls around Dr. Thorton's neck to the smudge of makeup on the collar of her silk blouse on up to her flickering eyelashes, which are heavily caked with mascara. She's oblivious to the camera recording the serene expression on her face and the look of defiance in her gray eyes, which are like two nails hanging Dr. Thorton's soul on the wall.

"You've left me no choice," Dr. Thorton says faintly, as she fumbles her pencil onto the floor.

"No choice but to lie," Pamela shoots back, this time aware that the camera is following her as she rises from her chair, cradling two notebooks in her left arm with the same degree of tenderness a parent uses when holding a child.

On celluloid the movement of Pamela's white slippers out of the doctor's office and down the corridor, at whose far end the elevator doors are closing, is synchronized with the sound track. There is silence, however, when she sits down in a red plastic chair and begins to leaf through her notebooks until she comes upon a passage, which she anxiously rereads while her thumb and forefinger keep folding and unfolding the upper right corner of the pages. Pamela feels the invisible eye penetrating the pores of her skin and deciphering the internal problem she is trying to resolve: whether she should transform the contents of her notebooks—which chronicle her experiences since leaving the *Chicago Tribune* a year ago—into a film script, or whether she should use the entries, interviews, and documents in her journals as the basis for a series of feature articles depicting her plight as a homeless person in San Francisco, who had been picked up by the police for public intoxication and bizarre behavior and involuntarily hospitalized in a psychiatric ward.

Pamela turned off her imaginary camera and spontaneously began to edit the pictures in her memory. She closed her eyes. The blank screen that seemed to shimmer in its stillness enticed her to reopen them. Suddenly she flashed that she could be both a director filming herself and a journalist; in her mind's eye she could direct the words into cinema, but on paper she would do what she did best: write articles exposing the corruption within the power structure of urban institutions. In Chicago she had earned a reputation as a hard-nosed investigative reporter when, after only two months at the *Tribune*, her series of articles revealed the people involved in a complex network of payoffs from bookmakers to the hierarchy of the Chicago Police Department. She had even earned the Chicago Journalistic Circle Award for that exposé. Also, as a result of her articles, the District Attorney's office handed up a series of indictments, some of which resulted in convictions that made it obvious, but not verifiable, that in addition to the slime found on policemen's hands, slick pockets were dripping with grease in city hall.

Recalling the impact of that exposé, Pamela became convinced that a series of articles based upon her experiences as a homeless person would be more immediately fruitful. Homelessness was a big issue, and Pamela knew that she had a story with national impact as well as a strong local hook. Urban corruption always sold newspapers, and the documentation she had assembled, not to mention her experiences, would have the journalistic force of a wrecking ball crashing into a straw hut. Besides, David Lawson, who had been an assistant editor at the *Tribune*, was not only an old friend of hers but three years ago he had moved to the Bay Area to assume the position of Features Editor at the *San Francisco Examiner*. Even though their only contact in the last three years had been exchanging Christmas and birthday cards, he and Pamela used to have lunch together at least twice a week and had often collaborated on important stories.

Still, there was one thing that worried her: San Francisco was not Chicago. In Chicago, the power structure of the city was on the surface, and like a frothing pair of shark's teeth, challenged you to defy it. But in San Francisco, the power structure was recondite; like an octopus, it would try to ravel around your neck from all directions if you discovered its hiding place. Once her initial fear subsided, Pamela became convinced that she need not be afraid of any repercussions her articles might have because she had the facts and the sources to substantiate them. Moreover, she knew that in the process of writing them she'd assemble the jigsaw puzzle that for the last year had been the shattered mirror of her life.

She closed her eyes and flicked the switch that whirred the camera of her memory. A photograph taken by her mother when Pamela was six months old spontaneously appeared. In the picture, the baby was smiling as she lay on her back on a changing table with her eyes fixed on a mobile that played "Brahm's Lullaby" while miniature teddy bears, hanging by strings from a rainbow, twirled around and around. The picture faded into a few slow-motion shots panning an empty room, which Pamela recognized as being the bedroom with a view of Lake Michigan, where she used to sleep with her ex-husband when they lived on Lake Shore Drive. Pamela opened her eyes trying to shake the picture from her consciousness; but even with her eyes open she could still see herself walking into her bedroom, aghast to discover her sister—naked except for a black hood over her head—leaning over Pamela's husband, whose wrists were handcuffed to the brass bedframe.

Other scenes began to whiz by: her tempestuous divorce and estrangement from her sister, her resignation from the *Tribune*, the nameless faces of the men she had picked up night after night in Rush Street bars when she was so drunk she could barely stand, the Bloody Marys she began drinking for breakfast, the straight shots of Jack Daniels she consumed for lunch, the bottles of cheap scotch she gulped down without benefit of a glass and which would end up scattered all over the Leavenworth Street apartment where she had lived when she first came to San Francisco, and the bottles of Night Train she used to ravenously drain when she lived in homeless shelters and on the streets.

Each scene was the ripple of an earthquake shaking her body. She could feel the pain knotting her muscles, could feel the despair moving like a claw over the inside lining of her stomach. Yet, emanating from the pain and despair that had shattered her self-image into a hallucinated demon she despised was a moment of prolonged lucidity at the end of which she knew how she'd begin her articles, because the tension all the scenes created had unleashed the words that would become the lead paragraph of her story: "Almost everyone has a way in which they either consciously or subconsciously try to destroy themselves. I chose an insidious but socially acceptable drug. Alcohol was the net that dragged me from a fashionable apartment on Chicago's Lake Shore Drive to the homeless alleys of Sixth and Mission in San Francisco."

The words, distilled from her memory and often filtered through shadows, kept pouring out. After a sleepless night in her room, during which she alternately stared at the stars through the panel of bars on the inside of her window and wrote, propped up by pillows in the corner of her bed, Pamela filled two memo tablets with a series of seven feature articles, which she already envisioned as the basis for a book. As the sun began to float toward the horizon on waves of orange and crimson, she felt immersed in an aura of self-confidence and serenity. It was all there on canary yellow paper. All that remained was to call up David Lawson and to produce an edited, typed version of what she had written.

Pamela laughed as she remembered the dazed expression on David's face after he had read her features on the Chicago Police. At first he'd been silent, as he sat back in his swivel chair and crossed his legs. Then, suddenly, his smooth, youthful face had become as animated as a room riddled by sunlight as he began telling her how impressed he was with the caliber of her writing and the way she had meticulously sourced her facts and situated the articles in a context that revealed the furtive machinery of Chicago politics.

In her imagination, she saw him reacting the same way again. David would also appreciate the fact that Pamela had inadvertently discovered the story when, as a member of the San Francisco Home-less Union, she had been assigned to edit a small mimeographed newspaper, which the union's executive board could use as both an organizing tool and a vehicle to put forward the union's program. Serious about her editorial responsibilities on the paper, Pamela had even quit drinking; and for the first time since the cacophony of her marriage and her subsequent descent into the labyrinthine fog of alcohol, she was finding a purpose for living and a sense of direction.

One day as she was editing an article for the paper, Steven Mauser, the president of the union, had asked Pamela to help him explore an enigma that had been puzzling him. Why was it, he wondered, that the Department of Social Services issued meal cards to homeless people that could only be redeemed at Saint Jerome's Church? Any why was it that when a card was presented at Saint Jerome's, it was taken, punched, and kept on file until the next time its owner returned? And why was it that when the person returned, holes were punched for meals that had never been eaten? After listening to Steven, Pamela's curiosity had been ignited.

Three weeks later, after she had assembled a mass of documentary evidence and conducted interviews with a number of sources who had revealed an elaborate network of kickbacks and payoffs at all levels of the city bureaucracy, her curiosity still wasn't satisfied. Despite the fact that she had a muckraking story that would send shock waves through city hall and make national headlines, Pamela knew there were people involved whose participation in an eight-million-dollar-a-year swindle of funds earmarked for the homeless couldn't be substantiated.

Yet that was the least perplexing of her problems. Pamela knew that sleaze always leaves an odor that clings, however faintly, to those who are involved in refining its machinations. She knew that one day the loathsome stench that all the poverty policemen and self-righteous politicians wallowed in would become so overpowering that it would inevitably suffocate them. But she also knew that the Fourth Estate, of which she herself was a member, emitted its own peculiar odor which was equally as nauseating. Often, in her more cynical moments when she was writing for the *Tribune*, she saw society as a palate whose taste buds are conditioned to uncritically savor media-prepared images as gourmet cuisine. In her more arrogant moments of unbridled self-importance, she fancied herself holding the rank of chef. This time, however, the story was too personal—and too proximate to the thin membrane of her psyche—to be spiced with pretense. It was not just a series of words stitched tightly together on deadline without any real regard for the human, soulful fabric and the deeper sociopolitical ramifications. But as personal as the story was to her, for editors it was just another story; and Pamela knew that stories were as ephemeral as the butterflies that children capture in mason jars.

Despite that, Pamela felt a resonating sense of responsibility. She also felt guilty, because unlike the homeless people among whom she had lived, she had access to a source of social power and privilege. Whether she liked it or not, she was a member of the Fourth Estate; she had the opportunity to translate human experience into words that millions of people could read and be moved by, and perhaps, if they were moved deeply enough, be compelled to translate their feelings and ideas into ameliorating social action. Still, as she sat on the corner of her bed looking at the words she had written the night before, Pamela felt compelled to destroy her articles because she was seized by an almost paralyzing fear that they would be received as an interesting sideshow in a media circus, and would ultimately have no impact other than to elicit the standard platitudes of outrage and compassion. But when she began to tear the pages in half, very slowly, and very conscious that her hands were shaking and her mouth was watering for a drink, she began to cry. Even though she had a particular disdain for the newsprint medium, her disdain for Saint Helena's and the depths to which she had plummeted was more overpowering. Journalism was her passport away from Napa; it was also her visa to a second chance at life—it provided the opportunity to disembark from the self-destructive journey upon which the poor self-esteem she had emblazoned onto the flammable map of her subconscious had taken her.

"I'm glad you finally came to your senses and called me," Lawson said sorrowfully, as he sat in the Sixth Floor North visitor's lounge listening to Pamela's reservations about herself and the media, after he had read her articles. "You know, of course, that what you have here is the type of dynamite that makes front pages explode. They'll eat this up on the wires faster than yuppies digging into a dish of gourmet ice cream."

Pamela half savored the tone in his voice. At the same time she struggled against being drawn into the undertow of the newspaper world, which flashed into her mind's eye as an unfathomable sea where crimson demons tinkered with the metaphysics of cynicism. The next day Lawson returned with a lawyer whose five-minute conversation with Dr. Thorton left the resident so red-faced and fidgety that her explanation to Pamela as to why she was being released from the hospital was as rapid as it was incoherent. As Pamela listened to the noise of the elevator's pulleys squeaking upward to 6-North, she felt a tingling warmth envelop her body, which rendered her slightly vertiginous. As she and Lawson walked out of the hospital into the sunlight that was seeping through the late afternoon fog, Pamela could see the camera capturing a close-up of the glass doors that, in black letters, bore the words "St. Helena's Neuro-Psychiatric Institute." She could sense the shadows from the swaying trees being captured on film as they glided across her face and cascaded onto the sidewalk. In her inner ear she could hear John Coltrane's "Ascension" accompanying the credits that were coming up on the screen.

She told herself that she should be elated. But her thoughts were electrical sparks that kept ricocheting off the revolving doors of her anxiety, and her eyes were oblivious to the camera that followed her to Lawson's car and captured a close-up of her hands buckling the seatbelt. When Lawson, his voice faintly audible above the noise of the motor, leaned over and asked her whether she would accept a job at the *Examiner*, Pamela could sense how the hidden eye was capturing the cynical smile that brought a blush to her cheeks, could sense how the tragedy that had been her life was dissolving into a melodrama. In her mind she couldn't help but be amused by the notion that the difference between tragedy and melodrama was the distance between Fifth and Mission, where the *Examiner* was located, and Sixth and Mission, where she had lived on the wine-glazed streets. As she began laughing hysterically, Pamela wondered how she was going to incorporate the next scene into the movie she was making of her life; wondered whether the memories of her odyssey for the past year and the agony that had left some of the corpuscles of her heart riveted to the cracked walls of homeless hotels would ever become as dim and insignificant as yesterday's byline.

Four Lives, Two Shelters

Renee Burgard

Debra and Christopher—New Life Shelter, Santa Cruz

Debra: "I was living in a house with some irresponsible roommates, and so I had the lease and utilities in my name. But then my back went out and I had to ask my roommates to leave, because they hadn't paid the rent in two months. So I felt totally lost. I stayed with various friends as long as I could, and then I called the Women's Crisis Center, and they suggested I call here. This was after I called every hotel and motel and discovered the only openings were like eighty dollars a night, and I couldn't afford eighty dollars a night. I couldn't afford eighty dollars a week. And so I called Women's Crisis and then I called here, and forty-five minutes later, here I was. It felt so good.

"I came at 9:30 at night, so I didn't meet many people that night, but the next day was church and I met quite a few people there. I never particularly cared for churches, but this one is really nice. You can feel the love in it. They have been fantastic to me. And my son loves it here. When I first came to the shelter, I envisioned all these trolls. When you think of the homeless around this area, that's what you think of. And I know a lot of people who aren't like that and they're homeless.

"I've been looking for another place, but I haven't found one yet. It's hard...my last place was $650 a month, and I had to pay close to two thousand dollars just to move in. I don't have that now. And I've had so much trouble with roommates, I really want a place by myself."

Christopher: "With me, though."

Debra: "Of course, honey. You'll go with me no matter what!

"Another thing is that a lot of people won't take children. I've heard that legally they're not allowed to do that, but I know they use every excuse not to give you the place if you have a child. Sometimes I just feel like pulling out all my hair. There's one girl here who's told me for the past three days, 'You're always smiling.' And I feel like if I stop smiling I might start to cry and I might not be able to stop."

Christopher—New Life Shelter, Santa Cruz

(When asked, "If there was one thing you could wish and have it come true, what would you wish for?")

"Well,…I'd wish that we could find a home to live in and then we could live happily ever after."

Anna and Sarah—Pajaro Valley Shelter, Watsonville

"I'd just moved here from Alaska and I was living in an apartment over on Fourth Street. A friend owed me a thousand dollars, and I was waiting for that, because I was working as a temporary for Kelly Services and it wasn't quite enough. So the check finally came and I put it in the bank, but then it bounced. On top of that, I had my paycheck stolen from me, right while I was walking to the bank. So there I was, with no money, the rent due, and checks I'd written using what turned out to be the bad check were all bouncing. I went to work and mentioned it to this guy, and he's Catholic and he knew about the shelter in Watsonville. So I contacted the shelter, and they told me they were full, but the next day they called and said they could give me a bunk bed. I gladly took it. I was seven months pregnant and working two part-time jobs and I was exhausted.

"People who go to that shelter, they're people who are coming from really traumatic situations—no place to live, no job, no food, or from a battering situation. They're not all people who are considered street people.

"As my thirty days came near, I finally found a place to share with another woman who said she would like to live with me even with my new baby. But then she chickened out and asked me to leave before Sarah was born. I found another room with an elderly lady, and I thought, 'Oh boy, this'll be great...' but I found out that she hadn't lived with anyone for a long time, and when Sarah came, she couldn't adjust. So she asked me to leave, too. I had to go back to the shelter, and the sisters were really helpful. They gave us some privacy, and I've just now been able to save up and start renting this place by myself. So now I'm just piecing it all together. And I'm pretty lonely sometimes, but the sisters at the shelter really became a part of my life and so I go over and see them a lot. And I'm finally making friends in the church. So things are working out. Sometimes I think I'm not very fortunate, and things are piling up, and I'm not going to be able to dig myself out. But as it turns out, we're pretty lucky actually. There are people a lot worse off. I can't imagine being in Africa and being a mother and watching my child die because I can't feed it. So we're fortunate. She's not malnourished by any means."

AIDS/ARC
and Homelessness

Dan Bellm

Less than two years ago, Paul* was earning a decent salary as a window dresser for a San Francisco department store. Then he was diagnosed with AIDS, and when he became unable to work, his entire world collapsed fast. He couldn't afford his rent of $450 a month, his disability insurance expired, and his roommate, who held the lease on the apartment, asked him to leave. As the first winter days of cold rain settled upon the city, Paul found himself sleeping at a city shelter, without a home.

Richard, an IV-drug user now in recovery, lost everything in a house fire a year and a half ago and ended up on the street. Three days later he was in the hospital with pneumonia; then he was diagnosed with AIDS-related complex (ARC). And he didn't know where he'd go, other than back on the street with a life-threatening illness, when it came time for the hospital to release him.

Mark used to work for Pacific Bell. Now he has PML, an AIDS-related nervous system disorder which has severely limited his motor control, and his workmen's compensation is about to run out. A month ago he could get around with a cane, but now he needs a walker, and his apartment is up a long flight of stairs. His roommate is getting tired of "dealing with this hospital atmosphere." Mark will have to move soon, but where?

Paulette, the mother of a sixteen-year-old son, has had cancer for three years; she's undergone several operations and another is coming soon. Two years ago, she found out she also had ARC. "I was honest with my roommate about my diagnosis," Paulette says, "but she couldn't take it. You find out who's a true friend and who's not.

Note: Some names have been changed in order to protect personal anonymity.

My family wasn't there. I felt devastated, forsaken—like a leper. I went to a hotel for three weeks and cried my eyes out. But I realized: I can't go on like this; my savings are going. What am I going to do?"

David, a sixty-year-old grandfather, is sitting in a hotel room surrounded by dozens of stuffed animals and remarkably, for a room only nine square feet, five of his friends. Two more visitors are standing in the doorway. There's a pot of coffee on, and Oprah Winfrey is on the tiny portable TV. David gingerly steps over to find another folding chair behind the door.

"I'm the elder of the group," he says, with a bright, campy smile. "Everyone calls me Granny." A former Navy nurse and a Korea and Vietnam veteran who first came to San Francisco in 1937, David was caring for his terminally ill mother in Oregon last year when he learned he had contracted AIDS from a blood transfusion. He has since come down with pneumocystis carinii, Kaposi's sarcoma, and leukemia.

"The day of my mother's funeral," says David, "my father kicked me out of the house. I came back to San Francisco, but I had no money and nowhere to live. For a while I stayed in a tent—not since Korea have I had so much fun. When it rained my tent filled up with water." Now he's at the badly run-down but friendly Folsom Street Hotel, managed as an AIDS/ARC residence by Catholic Charities. "We're a family," he says. "We extend a hand and try to help each other over the next step. We've been through it all and we understand."

❖   ❖   ❖

Since the AIDS epidemic began, San Francisco has been setting the worldwide standard for compassionate health care. But with fifteen hundred or more people with AIDS now living in the city, many are still falling through cracks in the system. Far fewer services, for instance, are available for the twenty-eight thousand or more people who are infected with the AIDS virus HIV, or who have developed ARC, but lack an official diagnosis of AIDS. And just when they most need a stable, clean, comfortable home, many are facing this disease alone—in temporary shelters, in miserable hotels, or on the street.

The city's Department of Public Health now estimates that two hundred to four hundred people with AIDS, ARC, or HIV infection are homeless in San Francisco; some healthcare workers set their estimates as high as six hundred. Dale Meyer, director of Catholic Charities' AIDS/ARC Program, foresees these figures doubling or tripling by 1993. But the programs that the health department helps fund can only house about 115 people; another 40 or 50 are housed informally in central city hotels.

AIDS service agencies daily watch the need for housing outpace the supply. The Shanti Project and Coming Home Hospice, which run residential programs for people with AIDS, receive about twenty requests a week, but the Shanti residences can only serve forty-seven people, and the Hospice's fifteen beds are reserved for people in the final stage of their illness. The San Francisco AIDS Foundation receives, on average, four or five applications a week for emergency housing; it provides one- or two-week vouchers for certain local hotels, and has one eight-bed flat where the maximum stay is six weeks.

Baker Place, a new AIDS/ARC residence for people in substance abuse treatment, can accommodate twenty-one people. Catholic Charities has recently bought a much better building to house thirty-two people, but Dale Meyer frankly admits this will cover "just a fragment of the need. Much, much more will have to be done."

City clinics find that a growing number of people coming in for AIDS care are unable to give a permanent address. Every night, at least two people with ARC or AIDS come seeking shelter at the ARC/AIDS Vigil, a tent-city protest which has camped out on blustery United Nations Plaza since October 1985. "Even considering an overlap in counting," notes Geoff Froner, a community health outreach worker with the MidCity Consortium to Combat AIDS, "this is an alarming situation."

San Francisco isn't alone. As far back as January 1986, the AIDS Shelter Project was already estimating that 28 percent of New York City's gay men with AIDS and 50 percent of its IV-drug users with AIDS were homeless.

"Discussions of homelessness tend to emphasize personal failure or mental illness," says Froner. "Anything to create a comfortable distance between 'us' and 'them.'" But a host of causes can lead people with ARC and AIDS, indigent and middle class alike, into poverty.

Extended periods of illness, sooner or later, mean a loss of employment. And anyone without substantial savings and a good insurance plan must "spend down" and become poor to qualify for public aid: General Assistance (GA) at $311 per month or Supplementary Security Income (SSI) at roughly $600. Becoming poor doesn't take long—one crisis or unforeseen expense can be enough to cause the plunge. And neither GA nor SSI can meet housing costs in San Francisco; even the most forlorn hotels cost $250 a month, and studios start at $400 or more—along with a deposit of an extra month's rent.

As a person's mobility wanes, apartments without an elevator or with dozens of stairs become unlivable. Some people are rejected—and ejected—by roommates, even by lovers or family members, out of fear. "The anomaly of an emaciated young man with a cane can be terrifying," says Froner. "It forces you to look at your own mortality."

Still others say that because of AIDS, they have been evicted or discriminated against by landlords, which is illegal but very hard to prove. Ramon, a man with AIDS who has a monthly insurance income of fourteen hundred dollars and can afford his own place, says he has been turned down by six landlords in three weeks of searching; the excuse they offer, he says, is that he's not holding a job. "My friends tell me to complain or take these people to court," says Ramon, "but I don't have the energy for that. I have to watch my own health."

Once AIDS or ARC has led to homelessness, the other half of the vicious circle emerges: homelessness drastically worsens one's health. Out-of-hospital health care becomes much harder to obtain, Kaposi's sarcoma lesions can't easily be soaked and soothed without a bathtub, and good nutrition habits falter without kitchen facilities. Shelters and welfare hotels spread more infections, and extended periods outdoors lead to more illness from exposure. Transportation is too costly. Money is harder to manage, and for someone using IV drugs, housing and food become secondary. Hospital stays become longer until, typically, a homeless person spends his or her last days there.

As an outreach worker, Froner does on-the-street AIDS-prevention education and counseling and hands out bleach and condoms to those at highest risk of infection—IV-drug users, blacks and Latinos, and homeless youth. Many street people who are already HIV-positive or have ARC, he's found, keep their health status a secret, not only to gain admittance to shelters but to avoid harassment on the street. Most of the AIDS/ARC housing programs can't serve substance abusers; what's left are the streets, the parks, or the revolving door of two- to five-day stays at "hotline" welfare hotels.

"What would I do in their situation?" muses Froner. "Hit a bank? Get high and live it up? I wouldn't have the energy. I'd end up in jail; then I'd die. So instead people just hang on and on this way."

"We're asking a lot from people on the street," says Harvey Maurer of the ARC/AIDS Vigil. "To change your sexual or drug behavior takes a lot of commitment and support. Reagan's 1988 State of the Union address didn't even mention AIDS. The Secretary of Education preaches abstinence: easy for him to talk. If society isn't committed to these people," he surmises, "why should they feel so committed to stopping the spread of this disease?"

❖ ❖ ❖

The Anglo Hotel sits next to the Jesus Saves Gospel Mission on an unlit corner of Sixth Street south of Market, a desolate strip where lost souls meet some of their hardest luck. A woman is mournfully yelling "Alvin!" over and over up to a closed window. A few men are killing time by the pay phone in the doorway, looking restless but beat.

The desk clerk behind the locked grille points to the "No Visiting Anytime" sign when I tell him Roger's room number. "So how am I supposed to see someone who lives here?" I ask. "There's no phone, there's no other way to reach him." "Okay," he scowls. "Five minutes."

Roger is lying across the bed in a ten-by-twelve-foot corner room up on the third floor, watching the TV someone loaned him, coughing into his pillow from time to time—a hard cough from deep in his chest. He's surprised I made it past the desk into "Fort Knox." Over six feet tall, with disheveled blonde hair and a welcoming grin, he looks tired and gaunt in his loose-fitting sweatshirt and jeans. He's just getting over the bout of pneumocystis that put him in San Francisico General for a few days and gave him a definite AIDS diagnosis after eight months of ARC.

Roger has been here for a couple of days through the hotline and has a couple of days more; he doesn't know where he's going next. The Episcopal Sanctuary, the shelter where he stayed before he got sick, is trying to find him a more permanent place, he says. He collects $139.85 on General Assistance every other week; he goes out only to see his doctor or to get meals at a church kitchen.

"This room is horrible," Roger says. He has stayed at many shelters and hotels over the past few months, but he calls this the worst. "I don't like to look around. I watch TV." There is nothing in the room but the bed, a tiny sink, a chest of drawers, and Roger's overcoat. The curtains are thin, limp, covered with yellow stains. The dusty red carpet is the kind that calls up images of smoke, and fire. The Anglo collects one hundred a week from the City for this room. "I don't even keep my clothes here," Roger says. "I don't want anything stolen. I keep them at a friend's house, half an hour away."

Roger came to San Francisco eight years ago from a small town in Ohio; he is twenty-seven years old. He has a three-year-old adopted son, whom he hasn't seen in two years, back in Ohio now with his ex-boyfriend. Roger used to work as a dog groomer and rented a studio apartment in the Castro district for $450 a month. After six months out of work because of ARC, he couldn't afford the place. Until two weeks ago, he had been shooting crystal methamphetamine for five years; he rolls up his right sleeve to show me the needle tracks. He still sees people shooting speed here in the halls and stairwells, he says, but pneumonia and AIDS have scared him so much now that "It's not so hard to quit. I don't want it any more.

"I'm past the self-destruction period," he goes on. "I want to keep living. But every day I'm amazed to wake up. My old friends aren't around. Most of my friends are dead—ten or twenty people in the past year. I figure I'm next, and I'm afraid of dying. But on the other side, sometimes I don't want to live because of the pain and torture."

"What keeps you going?" I ask. A decision to stay off drugs seems remarkable, heroic, given the circumstances. "Is there something you dream about?"

"I just want to go back to see my little boy," he answers with a hopeless, tender look.

While we talk, old reruns of "The Jeffersons" and "Cheers" have been playing on the TV, a black-and-white set with a constant blip. Roger chuckles infectiously at the programs now and then. "What shows do you like to watch?" I ask. "Anything nonviolent," he says. "Anything to keep a smile on my face."

"You do keep a great smile on your face," I tell him. He looks so stoic, so vulnerable. "Do you ever cry?"

"I cry all the time. It used to be I couldn't. A friend got me to cry

120

once. He said, let it all out. I got so scared I stopped, and then I started crying again. I cry all the time."

We sit in silence for awhile. There isn't very much to say. "You're nervous," Roger suddenly observes in a kind voice.

"Yes, I guess I am," I tell him bashfully. "I'm not used to being down on Sixth Street."

"No," says Roger. "Neither am I."

❖   ❖   ❖

Although San Francisco's homeless program has an annual budget of $7.5 million, about $5.9 million of it will be spent this year on short-term "emergency services," placing up to three thousand homeless people a night in shelters and in hotels like the Anglo. Meanwhile, the City's programs to create permanent housing, by rehabilitating vacant or abandoned units, are in line for severe budget cuts. Federal subsidies for low-income housing have already been cut by two-thirds in this decade under President Reagan. But to redirect money out of its emergency funds, the City would have to displace hundreds or thousands of people indefinitely from the hotels and shelters: another vicious circle.

Mayor Art Agnos began his term in January with a pledge to solve the city's crisis of homelessness. The crisis is staggering. A recent report estimated that the nine-county Bay Area has up to forty-eight thousand homeless people, but fewer than three thousand beds in its shelters. At least sixty-nine homeless people died in San Francisco in the first eleven months of 1987, forty-four of them out-of-doors.

An ad hoc housing committee, made up of representatives from the city's AIDS/ARC service agencies and many other community groups, has been meeting twice a month for over a year to monitor the situation and brainstorm a way out. Given the difficulty of creating new housing, the committee is calling on the city to implement at least a support structure for people with AIDS and ARC who are isolated in hotels. Minimal services, they say, should include rent subsidies, case management, and home health care. And chairperson Kitty Ryan, from the health department's Central Aid Station, points to three more groups whose housing needs remain largely unmet: HIV-infected families, HIV-infected single women, and the fifteen hundred to two thousand homeless youth [who] live on the streets of San Francisco."

121

But a new wave of activism has begun to turn up the heat. Several people a day continue to be arrested at the ARC/AIDS Vigil, chaining themselves to the doors of the old Federal Building on United Nations Plaza to protest what they call a national failure to address the AIDS crisis. Upstairs, overlooking the plaza, is the regional office of the federal Department of Health and Human Services.

Last December, HHS regional director George Miller reportedly referred to the Vigil as "those damned tents," adding, "I think they've proved their point. I can't tell them what to do, but in my opinion they should just declare victory and leave." That's not likely, says Harvey Maurer of the Vigil, until the victory includes "a national health care system in this country, and a national housing system, like in every other developed country on earth."

❖   ❖   ❖

When gay men and lesbians pick up the biweekly *Bay Area Reporter*, San Francisco's oldest gay newspaper, the first page many read is the obituaries, a ritual of marking who is gone now, which friend or neighbor, which familiar face from Polk or Folsom or Castro Street. Last October, this item appeared:

"Eddie 'E.J.' Jolly and Clyde 'Joanie' Tatro were Tenderloin street partners and constant companions. They died on August 28, within hours of each other, but not within reach of each other. E.J. was in Saint Luke's Hospital, and Joanie in their hotel room. They did not die in the arms of loved ones, but alone and separated, not only from each other but also from those of us who cared for them and tried to help them as they struggled with the problems of poverty, homelessness, and AIDS-related illnesses during their last few years....
"They cared deeply for those around them in the Tenderloin, especially for Terri, who died in December 1986, also on the streets....
"We have all been touched by knowing them. In their name we will fight for the rights of all people with AIDS and ARC to die with dignity."

The Homeless Envelope

David Plumb

The fat yellow manila envelope
on the window ledge of the Bank of America
branch at Stockton and Columbus
said Harry Woodson, homeless
The poor state of his life attested to
by a dental clinic sheet with a bus token taped on
that would get his teeth fixed
or at least the front right incisor he complained about
saying he was a volunteer in their food program
and according to another form
he was supposed to have a welfare interview at ten
to prove beyond a shadow of a doubt
that he was Harry Woodson and that he
lived at the Holland Hotel

I called his case worker
A Filipino man who talked too fast
and got ground up on the phone with the buses going by
and when I rang the Holland Hotel bell
I was greeted on the stairs by a woman named Patel
who was suspicious of me, of him and I'd guess the world in general
At any rate he'd checked out
and I had the envelope

A documentation of hunger
one-night stands and rotting teeth,
suspicion, alienation, and missed appointments
A fragmented life trying a piece at a time
to make sense, to get it right, to get to the bus stop
with what little ammunition he had left
(yes he was a vet) to take the token
before losing it to a stranger or a crowd
before the madness took over or the tooth hurt too much
or the bus went by
and the bus went by
and all that was left was the envelope
I put back on the ledge

Intimacy

Jean Vengua Gier

He's sleeping in the public library again,
sunken into a green vinyl chair.
Mouth sagged open, his breath draws in
and out in slow sucks, like an infant's.

His trousers and shirt are baggy, clay
colored; his hair is shaved close to the
scalp. Black, scuffed funeral shoes enclose
his feet, no socks—the pale skin
exposed, gently covering the medial bones
of his ankles.

3 o'clock—a summer heat wave settles
its sediment over the town. But he's far off,
lungs opening, gathering breath to the belly of
a dream, which fills him with its milk. He is
content with this public bed. His left hand

is thrust down within the fly of his
trousers, and closes limp upon the warm
cave of his groin, with its soft
and recumbent tools.

We, who are awake, browse past innocent—each
turns away with a gift: rage, or a mute stone
at the lips. We turn, as if from the coffin,

and move slowly about the rooms, like boats
trawling a still, windless sea, hands
reaching out to touch the cloth
or paper bindings.

Barefoot

Allen Cohen

Walking down Columbus Avenue
passing the bronzed fire-fighting heroes
I saw a young derelict with bearded
and clouded face walking,
his arm outstretched as if frozen,
in the midst of a soliloquy –
he was dressed in Salvation Army
oversized clothing but he was barefoot.
His red feet were swollen to twice
their normal size due to gout
or arthritis and he shuffled
as if walking on boards.
A block further I passed
an older man steaming
and red with winefire –
his feet also bare and swollen.
And I remembered a third man
who sleeps in the Panhandle
in the sun by day (who knows
how he survives the night?) –
he wears layers of baggy clothes
and his hair is long and matted,
both his hands and feet
are naked and swollen.

In 1966 & '67 young bare feet
of boys and girls walked
San Francisco's asphalt streets
defiant with the austerity of youth
in imitation of earthwalkers,
holy men and Amerinds.

These same feet now jog
in sixty-dollar Adidas
thru the streets and parks.

On Brooklyn waterfront 1962
I remember the winos I let steal
wine and brandy from liquor store
I worked in—their feet and hands
red and swollen but wrapped
in any rag they could find,
bundles of rags warmed
their feet against icy winters.
Each cold morning they came
to me with small change
and lowered eyes and
told me who had frozen
under old newspapers
in dark underground cellars.

caves." Down there they had mattresses, blankets, and pots and pans that they cooked in over a jerrybuilt brick barbecue, the grating of which was an oversized iron window-trellis that doubled as a table where its ends stuck out over the fire pit. Old Max even had a portable radio and a small library of paperbacks.

This was the third night that Mark and Bill had slept in the caves, and now they were sitting around, gabbing over morning coffee, passing a fifth of tokay between them, then over to old Max, each taking a long, slow swallow when it was his turn. They each wore an old overcoat, which was stuffed with newspapers for warmth and which they slept in, and each drew a dirty old blanket around his shoulders to keep out some of the early morning chill and dampness.

"It could well be that there *are* fads and fashions in the wino world," Bill continued. "Some of those dashers up on the corners who sashay up to Aquatic Park or Buena Vista, those guys might set the styles, say what's in and what's out. And you can just see how it works: the popularity of a particular brand then spreads by word of mouth via the grapevine—through County Hospital detox wards, the drunk tank and the city slammer, on over to Saint Anthony's Dining Room, and so on. I can just see it: there's this magazine called *Wino World* and in it are distinguished, classy-looking winos, looking like Mark maybe, and they give testimonials on its pages. '*I get more from life with Franzia White.*' It's touted as going with every brand of butt you could find on the street today. '*It takes the slaps out of the DTs.*' They say it '*steadies the Bull Durham-rolling fingers, enabling you to get that rise-and-shine smoke with a little dignity.*' Well, don't you ever wonder about who sets these fads?"

Mark, whose mood that morning was far from jovial, took advantage of Bill's rhetorical question to attack him testily. "It's us, Bill, you and me, that's who. You and me and Max, and Bill the Dude, and all of the others—we're all one of a kind. And all of us, and that includes you, are here to stay—you'd be a lot better off just accepting that idea.

"You used to be a college professor; I used to own a discotheque in London. So what? Max is sixty-three, you're forty-eight, I'm forty-one, and we'll all probably die living like this." Of cirrhosis maybe, maybe under the wheels of a bus, or in the detox ward, what difference does it make? We ought to quit kidding ourselves, you and me.

"We're here to stay, Bill, let's face it. It's you and me who set any trends, all your joking aside. But if the idea that what you do affects

128

us all—even if it's just what we drink—will inspire you to comb that stringy mop of yours, sew a couple of buttons on that old rag overcoat of yours, or keep your ass a bit cleaner, then it's worth consideration."

"If you weren't such a limey fruit, Mark, I might land a good one right on your nose. But it might kill you, so I won't. I don't know what's got into your craw today, but c'mon, let's get up on the street and get some of those commuter quarters. Somebody's got to see that we don't all die down here."

The two of them walked up to the street, leaving their bottle of tokay with Big Max.

Mark was panhandling on the corner of Seventh and Mission, almost on the curb edge in order to catch the heaviest foot traffic at the light crossing, when an old, mag-wheeled Chevy slowed to a stop in front of him. A young guy in the front passenger side thrust something out at him without saying a word and without moving his head far enough below the top of the window for Mark to get a look at his face; then the car sped off. Mark found himself bobbling a leather satchel in his hands. Dumbfounded, wondering what had happened, he automatically started across the street to where Bill was panhandling catty-corner from him. On the way he started to unzip the bag to find out what was in it. Bill saw him coming across the street and began jabbering, talking to him as though he had been locked in a solitary cell for a week, yelling at him across the street.

"Mark, old boy, you know what we two ought to do? We ought to do the same thing the monarch butterfly does in the winter—fly south to Mexico. We could hitchhike there, spend the winter with the butterflies." Mark was stepping up on the curb in front of Bill. "You know, butterflies from all over go down there, from the East coast, all the way down from Canada. They travel thousands of miles and meet there, in a forest outside Mexico City. Millions of them. They turn the tops of the trees solid orange, there's so many. They just sit up in those trees all winter long, not moving, not eating, not doing anything, just resting, getting it all together. Then, in the springtime, when they head north again, they're refreshed. They're saved from this unnatural, life-sapping kind of cold and wet that drains our best energies and makes us too weak to cope like men. I tell you, Mark, that's what you and I ought to do. Fly away south and get ourselves together again..."

"Take a look inside this thing, Bill. Open it up." Mark pushed the brown satchel at Bill, explaining how it had been thrown at him just minutes before while he was panhandling.

Bill unzipped the satchel a couple of inches, then closed it back up. "Jesus Christ, Mark. How much do you think there is? Looks like nothing smaller than hundred-dollar bills to me. Lots of 'em. Christ almighty."

"What are we going to do with it, Bill?" Mark was worried.

"Well, let's start by taking one of those bills over to Ralph's and getting ourselves a couple of bottles. Then we better get this bag back to the caves and think this over."

At Ralph's Liquors, Bill picked out two fifths of the best wine on the shelves, Sauvignon Beaulieu. Then Mark handed Ralph a one-hundred-dollar bill.

"Where in the hell you guys steal that?" Ralph asked as he tugged at the two ends of the bill as though he expected to snap it in two.

"Hell, Ralph, Mark's mother over in England finally answered one of his letters. You know, they finally came across with some cheese, like he's been trying to get them to do for a couple of years. Finally felt sorry for him getting so screwed up and all and signing all his money over to one of those Buddhist monasteries, or whatever it was. They finally forgave him."

"Well, I don't know what in the hell you're hangin' around here for, then. I heard you were from some upper crust family, but I never believed it." Bill grabbed up the bag with the wine in it and reached over for the change Ralph was counting out for Mark, trying to cut short the conversation.

"Well, take it easy drinkin' that stuff. Ya might kill yourselves on it, you two been drinkin' that kerosene so long."

On their way back to the caves, Mark and Bill discussed the money. It was probably hot, they figured, and if they got caught with it they might just end up taking the rap for it. On the other hand, they figured, if the bills weren't recorded, and if the guy who threw the satchel out of the car wasn't nabbed, they were home free with a whole lot of money. As they walked back up Mission and over to the caves on Howard Street, they agreed to hide the satchel from Big Max. When they got back they explained the fancy wine to him as a celebration over the fact that Mark had panhandled a ten-dollar bill that morning. Scoring that much happened so rarely that when any of the winos claimed it did, it was understood to be a tall tale. Big Max didn't question them about it, and they opened the corked bottles with his Swiss army knife and passed them around to him.

The wine was bitter to their taste. They had become used to the heavy, sweet tastes of tokay, sherry, and tawny port. Mark and Bill had forgotten how sour good wine could taste. Big Max grumbled that they should have got a bottle of brandy instead. He would only drink from what was left of the bottle of tokay he had from the morning. As Mark and Bill sat around drinking, they each knew that the other's thoughts were on the satchel. Bill thought about how they could buy themselves a whole new life with what was in that satchel hidden under Mark's mattress.

The next morning Mark and Bill got up earlier than usual. Not even drinking morning coffee with Max, they hurried on up to the newsstand two blocks away. There, half-way down the front page of the morning paper, they saw the story they were looking for:

Midget Murdered
—MISSING 200-Gs STASH—

A 31-year-old Hillsborough midget, "Little" Harold DeWarcusi, was strangled to death in a Mission district Safeway parking lot while his 320-lb, 5-ft-10-in father was inside shopping for groceries.

DeWarcusi's father, known as Baron DeWarcusi, had just come from the bank where he had the family's savings converted into one-hundred-dollar bills which he then stashed in a brown leather satchel.

DeWarcusi left the satchel on the front seat of the car with Harold when he went into the Safeway. He came back to the car to find Harold had been strangled with a cowhide belt which was still tied around his neck. He was underneath the car dashboard. The satchel was missing.

"Little" Harold DeWarcusi, a former circus performer with Ringling Brothers Circus, came to the U.S. from Hungary as a youth to travel with the circus. He was billed as the "world's littlest man" at 2 ft 9 in tall. His mother, a bearded lady, and his father had also come over from Hungary to join the circus.

The DeWarcusis were planning to close a deal to sell their million-dollar Hillsborough home next week and return to Hungary to live.

Further on, the article announced:

DeWarcusi and his wife refused to discuss what had happened or to be photographed. Their only statement was that they didn't want the incident to get in the way of their plans to leave the U.S. The FBI questioned them for over an hour yesterday afternoon.

Neighbors said that the DeWarcusis had grown reclusive over the past year. "Little" Harold hadn't spoken to anyone in the neighborhood of ornate Spanish style homes for more than a year, although he was often seen out in the yard with the family Doberman Pinscher.

"Well, there's where our loot came from, Mark. The bastards. They didn't have to kill the little guy. Christ, they could have tied him up, a guy that size. Poor little guy. Somebody like that wouldn't have a chance in hell against a guy our size. There ought to be more police protection in a city like this. Used to be you could walk around on the streets and not have to worry about getting mugged, or murdered. Now I wouldn't trust myself to sit down in a doorway anywhere in this city.

"Looks like we're free and clear with the money, Mark old boy. None of those bills were marked, the guy just got them from the bank and stuffed them in that bag, and it doesn't even look as if they even give a damn whether they get it back or not. The guys who did it must have panicked, probably didn't intend to get involved in a murder. What do you want to do, Mark? I'm for heading for Mexico right now, the two of us, down to Acapulco, then Mexico City, then maybe Europe. We can do anything now, anything we want to do. No more scrounging around on Howard Street. We can live anywhere in the world now."

Mark was thoughtful and slow to say anything. "I bloody well know that *we* can," Mark finally said, "but what about the others? What about Bill the Dude, and Ice Cream Charley, Harry, and Big Max? Aren't we going to give them some of it? After all, if Max hadn't invited us to stay with him in the caves, we might not have been up on Mission Street, probably wouldn't have, not that early in the day anyway, and we wouldn't have gotten the money in the first place. Max has taken good care of us, too."

Something about the tone of Mark's voice irritated Bill even more than the stupid things he was saying.

"There you go again, you limey marshmallow. Those caves are open to anybody who wants to carry a mattress down there or who has the guts to adopt one of the old ones already there. It's city property, Max doesn't own it. Anybody can stay there, so don't give me that crap. And how do you know we wouldn't have been pan-handling right there where we were yesterday morning? You're not clairvoyant, there's no way you could predict what would have happened to us yesterday, so don't even try. What happened just happened. Coincidence, pure coincidence that we stayed with Max the night before. As for the others, they didn't have a damned thing to do with our windfall, and you know it."

Mark lapsed into a kind of quavering speech, almost bordering on a whine. "But it could just as easily have been one of the others that this happened to, and we would feel rotten if we found out about it and they didn't share at least a little of it with us. Old Max is sick, too, he could use a trip to a doctor for his stomach, and Bill the Dude doesn't have a tooth left in his head to chew his food. I don't see how it could hurt to give all of them some, at least a small cut."

"Jesus, you're naive, Mark. For a guy who has been around money most of your life, you don't know much about it. You're soft, and you're gutless, too. The only reason you were ever successful in that business of yours back in London was because you had a lot of money backing you up and a lot of rich friends to keep the place going. You'd never have made it if you had had to fight your way to the top."

Bill could see he was going to have to convince Mark, and he meant to do just that, any way he could. "First of all," Bill argued, "how would we decide how much to give the other guys? Suppose we _were_ to cut them in, say just the other four, give them each, say, a thousand bucks. Are they going to be able to keep it quiet? Not on your life. All of a sudden four old winos get new overcoats, their hair is cut and combed, they're cleaned up, and they're flopping up in the Planters Hotel instead of under Howard Street or in one of the missions or in the drunk tank, like usual. How is that going to look? Mighty suspicious. And each of them is buying all this stuff with one-hundred-dollar bills. It would take about two days before the whole city police force, the FBI, and the CIA for that matter, were down here investigating. And I don't have any desire to look at the inside of a jail cell for twenty years. Besides, think about it. All those guys would do with that money is buy themselves hard liquor for a couple of months, until the dough ran out. They'd kill themselves right now on booze if they could afford to. Sure, they'd move up to some of the hotels on Mission for a while, maybe eat a little more than they do now, but not much because all they really want are the spirits. Then where would they be in about five months, when the dough ran out? What makes you think Old Max would even bother going to a doctor, or Bill the Dude to a dentist? Did you think of that? You know damn well they'd be right back down here again, and worse

133

off than they were before.

"The other guys, they're not like you and me, Mark, they don't *think*, and they've got nothing to go back to, no other home but the street, the caves, the drunk tanks, and the detox wards. So don't start complicating this thing. Let's just split the money and leave quietly. We can both get ourselves together, get back into the real world where we belong. You know—we both know—that there's something better than this. You could even go back to England now and start another business."

Mark seemed almost to have caved in to Bill's forceful logic. Now he looked resigned and depressed, but at the same time strangely frightened. He talked as though he were arguing for his life, rapidly, and with a stiffened emotion charging his voice.

"I'm never going back there. That business and everything else in my life was something my mother forced on me, it was all something she wanted for me. I hated it and everything it stood for. When I left, I left to start a new life. I presumed that I could leave my family, my business, and my friends all behind me. And I did, in a way, except that I never was very much of a person on my own without all of those props. They were more me than anything I could ever be on my own; I guess they really were all I ever was. That's why it was so easy for the right person to take advantage of me. You're very right, I don't know anything about money, or living either; at least I didn't until I wound up down here a year and a half ago.

"Now I know at least a little about some things," Mark went on quickly, "about eating and sleeping and protecting myself from the cold and rain. I know that I'm a disgraceful failure in the eyes of the whole world, and most of all in the eyes of my mother, but I'm just beginning to become someone separate from those material props that used to be the only me there was. Now I've learned to exist entirely without all those props, and however pitiful my existence may seem to everybody else, no matter how degrading, no matter how people may look at the rags I'm wearing, and no matter how repulsed they might be by what they see as the filth I live in, I am, in some small corner of my being, becoming me, learning to be *someone*, a real person with genuine feelings and thoughts and inspirations all my own. Can you possibly understand that?

"I've spent most of my forty-one years despising the absence of myself, the littleness that was my soul. Now at least I can tolerate myself. Someday I might think of going back to that world if I still could, but it wouldn't be for a long time. This past year has been the happiest in my life, Bill, believe it or not—if I have *ever* experienced happiness at all, and I don't know if I have yet. I'm just now earning my right to live, finding myself, finding the personal thoughts and emotions that should have been mine naturally."

Bill interrupted him angrily. He couldn't believe what he was hearing, and he didn't want to hear any more of it. It rankled him in a way he couldn't quite explain, and he didn't want to be forced even to listen to what Mark was saying, much less to have to think about it.

"You're going to *take* your half of that money, Mark. This is the biggest thing that ever happened to me in my life, and I want to leave here knowing that I don't have to worry about you spreading this story all over where the cops or the FBI might catch wind of it. What if they trace that satchel to you? You're going to come out of town with me, to Mexico, as soon as we get ourselves cleaned up and get some new clothes, or I'll kick your ass 'til you do. So don't try to argue with me about it, it's settled." This time Mark didn't even try to answer him. Bill knew he had succeeded, had overridden Mark's objections, at least to the extent that Mark would now do what Bill wanted him to do. Bill took charge of the situation and started planning their next moves aloud, ignoring Mark's indifference to everything he was saying.

Bill got the two of them a room in a Sixth Street hotel where they could shower, shave, and put on the new clothes Bill had bought for them at the Purple Heart Thrift store with the change from the first hundred-dollar bill. Bill pulled a long drink from the Hennesey cognac he had bought, passing it to Mark from time to time and hurrying him along while he showered, shaved, and dressed, patting him on the back every so often.

"Mark, you look like a million dollars, never knew you were such a handsome guy. Let's hurry it up now and get down to the Wharf. We're gonna celebrate first, have a big seafood dinner in Joe DiMaggio's restaurant on the pier. Break a couple more of those hundred-dollar bills."

While Mark was in the shower, Bill first transferred about a thousand dollars of the money from the satchel into a wallet he had bought along with the clothes. He then wrapped up some of the hotel

135

ash trays in newspaper, to displace the weight he took out, putting them into the satchel. The rest of the money he put into a double Safeway shopping bag, which propositioned the world in big red letters: "Since we're neighbors, let's be friends." Bill planned to give Mark the satchel to carry until he could find somewhere along the wharf to throw it into the bay, where he could be sure no one would find it. He would carry the shopping bag himself.

It was hard to tell where Mark's head was now, because Mark had stopped talking to him. He was silent, almost morose, and he moved only when Bill told him to. He was acting just like a child, Bill thought, like a spoiled kid who couldn't have his way.

When they were both finally ready to go, they looked indistinguishable from any other two businessmen on the city streets. Bill put the satchel into Mark's hands and then propelled him towards the door to get him to leave the hotel.

They had just swung off the cable car and were walking down the long steep hill toward the pier when Mark broke his silence, muttering a phrase, in a voice that was barely audible, that sounded to Bill like, "the midget was the only one..."

Suddenly Mark bolted away down the street. Bill gave chase, holding tight to the Safeway bag, but Mark was much quicker, younger, and in much better physical condition. Bill watched, helplessly, huffing and with a pain in his side, as Mark opened the driver's door of one of the cars that were creeping slowly down the hill toward the water. Mark grabbed the occupant of the driver's seat and in one quick jerk, ripped the man out of his car and threw the satchel into the back seat. Then Mark jumped into the driver's seat and hit the gas pedal, so that the car took off with a jolt toward the pier. Bill ran after it as fast as the pain in his side would allow him.

When he got down to the end of the pier, Bill could see the car where it had landed in the bay, about thirty feet from the end of the pier. It had landed upright in the water and was now sitting there, floating, just beginning to sink. The rear end was going down first. Mark was sitting up in the front seat. The people out on the end of the pier were screaming, yelling, and pleading with Mark to open up one of the doors and get out of the sinking car before it was too late. But Mark, who was smiling and waving to the onlookers, just sat, smoking a cigarette and making no move to escape.

Bill could see Mark still smiling as the back end of the car steadily slipped down into the oil-slicked bay; then the front end of the car took a sudden heave and lifted once as it sucked water under the engine compartment and disappeared completely. Five minutes after the car had sunk, the police arrived. They talked to the bystanders, and Bill heard them radio back to police headquarters for a diving team to recover Mark's body.

Bill tightened his white-knuckle grip on the Safeway bag and slowly walked back up the hill to the cable car turnaround. The words of an old song his father used to sing kept running over and over in his head...It was a song his father and his jobless cronies had sung outside the doors of Salvation Army missions during the depression:

> Oh, why don't you work like other men do?
> How the hell can I work when there's no work to do?

> Hallelujah, I'm a bum again, Hallelujah,
> Give us a handout, revive us again

> Oh, I love my boss and my boss loves me,
> And that is the reason that I'm so hun-gry

> Hallelujah, I'm a bum again, Hallelujah,
> Give us a handout and revive us again

> Oh, I went to a house and I asked for some bread,
> A lady came out, says, "The baker is dead"

Juana Alicia

The Blue People Report

Bob Wakulich

According to Brad Portnoy, a civic waste management engineer and close neighbor of Nat Hucktussle, Nat's major claim to fame used to be the unusually high number of his magazine subscriptions. Many people—Nat's letter carrier included—contend that Hucktussle must be receiving almost every periodical available in North America. Notable exceptions are *Solid Wastes Management, The Journal of Refuse Removal,* and *Sewage Works Monthly.* He borrows these religiously from Portnoy and reports that he finds the political sympathies of the editors highly amusing. The issues are often returned within twenty-four hours, well thumbed but never abused.

No one in the neighborhood doubts that Nat actually reads all the publications he gets. In public, he is rarely seen without at least one magazine in his hand and others jammed into the side pockets of one of his many tattered sportscoats.

BRAD PORTNOY: "I invited him over to watch a Stanley Cup game once, but he shook his head and said there were some things he had to read. My brother-in-law says that means he's gay, but I figure it's just...I dunno, maybe he drank something from under the sink when he was a kid."

None of Nat's neighbors are in agreement about why he reads so much. Some find it strange, or even scary. Others are philosophical: some people jog, some collect stamps, Nat reads magazines. The only thing most of them agree on is that his incredible appetite for glossy pages has never stopped him from being misinformed.

On one occasion, Nat stood up from his usual stool at a local diner, swallowed the last bite of a club sandwich, angrily pushed his metal-rimmed glasses back up his nose, and loudly blamed a recent spell of bad weather on a growing cartel of communist beekeepers. It was all right there in the magazines, he assured them, if they knew how to read between the lines. Another time, he ranted that there was mounting evidence that mayors and other civic officials across the country were breaching federal law by keeping nuclear waste in doghouses in their backyards.

Needless to say, when Nat announced over lunch one day that there were blue people living in his garage, most of the diner patrons nodded politely and went back to their cheeseburgers and beef dips. It wasn't until virtually everyone in the neighborhood had a similar problem that people began to take Nat more seriously. And now that these blue people—commonly referred to as "blues"—are popping up in garages and carports across the nation, Nathaniel Philbert Hucktussle has assumed the position of unofficial leader of the anti-blue movement.

The blues are refugees from fact-finding spaceships sent from Cyania, a small, unassuming planet in a neighboring galaxy. When the first ships landed some six years ago, the blues were well prepared to handle initial inquiries. Aroni Mac, a former Cyanian ship captain and early defector, admits that they managed to elude heavy publicity by the use of a simple but effective deception.

ARONI MAC: "Back then, when any of your people appeared, our people would begin shouting out things like *'We're losing our light, people!'* or *'Where the hell is Continuity?'* Then I would walk over and tell them we had all the extras we could possibly use, but if they promised to keep it quiet, we could slip them into the crowd scene. After about six months, we had over four hundred of you running through a field, screaming and carrying on.

"Unfortunately, a few people got in touch with the actors' union. One of the reps showed up and threatened to shut us down unless everybody got standard rates and on-site catering. We told him it was a student production, but it was only a matter of time before we were found out."

After some preliminary shock, the world was quick to accept these intergalactic explorers, especially after a number of early diplomatic exchanges indicated that their weapons were better than ours. Subsequent meetings revealed that the blues meant us no harm, coming here only to observe our ways and study our technological advances.

Aroni Mac: "We were very much impressed with the fact that you people could put ketchup, mustard, relish, and vinegar into those cute little plastic packets. What a concept.

"On the other hand, we were shocked with how you use tobacco—although the way you package it is great, just ideal for dips and fondues."

Nat Hucktussle: "I remember meeting one at a garden party back before they started squatting by my Studebaker. It was kind of dark and I was pretty wazooed, and I didn't know he was blue until he asked me for a cigarette and then ate it. He asked me for another one, and I said I only had a couple left. That's when he got all huffy and said, 'You'd have one for me if I weren't blue.' I felt kind of guilty at first, but then I started thinking that they could say that kind of thing no matter what you did, so why bother?"

Our own studies show little physical difference between blues and ourselves. Except for some fundamental philosophies, food preferences, and their habit of sleeping by day, only their color distinguishes them from us.

Brad Portnoy: "If you stayed out of the sun and ate a pack or two of cigarettes a day, what color do you think you'd be?"

After a while, many blues began cashing in their Cyanian gold dust allocations and spending their days off engaging in Earth activities. They became regulars at boutiques, delis, and espresso cafes. They went to movies. They learned the latest dances. When these excursions were cut back to one day a month, signs of discontent began to surface among the crews.

Aroni Mac: "There were the usual complaints of extraterrestrial research groups. The living quarters were cramped, the food was pretty lousy unless we ordered take-out, there was never enough tobacco, and nobody could get pay TV. Then there were research department cutbacks and longer shifts, and things got even worse."

Blues began to wander away from their ships about two years ago, most of them claiming that they needed some air. At first, patrols were formed to look for them and bring them back, but for every one they tracked down, another three wandered off. Then the research ships were suddenly recalled to Cyania, leaving hundreds of blues to fend for themselves.

In the beginning many of them wandered the streets, spending their nights looking for cigarette butts and handouts. Some people were sympathetic, others chased them away. With the help of makeup and fake IDs, some of them got work at all-night gas stations and convenience stores.

Government leaders sent appeals to Cyania, only to be told that their Earth investigation project was now complete. As far as they were concerned, the strays could go jump.

ARONI MAC: "We're not asking for much. You have a very nice planet here, and all we need is a little tobacco and a place to sleep. We figured you wouldn't mind if we used your garages."

NAT HUCKTUSSLE: "It wasn't really that bad at first. There were only two of them, and they offered to pay rent, and my car ashtrays were always spotless. Then more arrived, and after a while I could hardly get my car in the garage. Then one of them piped up that I hadn't been smoking much lately and maybe they should get a break in the rent. That was it, I figured, and I kicked the whole bunch of them out.

"It turned out there were some other people having the same problem, so we got together and formed a sort of a club. We exchange information, and I put out a newsletter on how to blue-proof your home.

"Look, it isn't that we don't like blue people or anything. I like 'em fine, but not in my garage. Next thing you know, they'll be turning up in our bloody closets."

In some circles it is feared that this has all the earmarks of a potentially explosive social problem. Blue jokes are being heard more and more at taverns, and proposed blue aid programs are not being well received in these tight economic times. In the final analysis, this is not a good time to be blue.

Love Poem
of the Orphaned Hobo

Alfredo Quarto

He came upon her in the alleyway,
her clean sheets spread
upon the down of her bed.
He saw the bare curves of her shoulders,
the smooth nape of her long neck,
her silken hair undone
around her sleeping form turned in
upon the fluff of pillow.
She breathed gently
in the night, out the day.
He stared for a moment trying to remember
who he was...
where he was,
rubbing his blood eyes in disbelief...
this could not be real,
this vision of the woman
whose features were as soft
as the ruff of newly fallen snow.
She was a fallen angel asleep amid the bottles
and debris, the old newspapers stained
with mud and wet of rain and piss and pain.
He staggered and nearly fell
but found support by leaning against her bedpost
of fine-carved mahogany
rounded and smooth to his touch,
cool, and he ran his rough fingers
along its veined column.
All the time he could not
take his eyes from her.
She became his sleeping beauty

and he the drunken prince of charm.
He cast off his old clothing
like a sailor might cast off to sea,
leaving all vestiges of things
familiar and near behind.
With his shirt he struggled cursing,
fighting to retrieve his arms
from the confines of cloth,
ripping the already torn sleeves.
His old boots with holes
like gaping eyes with toes
staring out in cold rejection
were kicked away from him
to land with their lapping tongues in snow.
The pants with the torn pockets and frayed cuffs
stained and seasoned with the months of use,
he pulled down around his knees
then sat to remove one worn leg after the other...
his bare skin now all goose flesh against the cold.
He turned toward her again
just to be certain she was there still,
his eyes followed the outline of her woman
curves under sheets beneath the glow
of yellowed street lamps and falling snow.
He lifted the covers to let himself in,
discovered sweet warmth beside her...
held her gently close to him.
She was like a rose,
an unfolding of petals drawing him near,
he fell asleep within her arms,
fulfilled with the scent of the flower of dreams.

       ◊   ◊   ◊

So, they were found next day,
their frozen forms enrapt in love in snow.
It was early morning and the paperboy
yawning the news to the world,
came across them.
Though his papers were filled with the headlines

depicting cities in ruin, earthquakes and wars,
political lies and far cries of social injustice,
of a murdered seamstress whose fate had been sewn
to the vagrant winds of some hideous crime—
a patchwork of mismatched realities
stitched there together in black and white
for all the world to see,
still the boy in all the few years of his youth
had never known that the mask of death
could ever be worn so smooth by a lost man...
and his lovely mannequin.

Photographs

Jean-Marie Simon

California Condor

David Olsen

This man defies all estimates of age,
And seems to have no name, or need of one.
He shuffles, mute, in tongueless tennis shoes,
Army surplus coat, and ragged dungarees.
The scraggly beard and hair so nearly match
His sun-scorched skin, that his cheeks
Trail off into matted fringe that hides his mouth;
Red coals glow with wild light where eyes should be.

With no address, he lives nowhere, everywhere.
He forages The Embarcadero
From China Basin to the Ferry Building.
On good days, the coin-return slots
Of newspaper vending racks can yield
A few quarters that missed the lock boxes.
On good days, the grocery clerk fails to see
The pocket's bulge, a can of Spam: tallow
For the candles behind his haggard eyes.
On good days, he sleeps in the sun
On a concrete bench, his arms flung wide
As if to embrace a tide that has receded
And left him stranded, mired in a mud flat
Like a worn, discarded tire.
On good days, stockbrokers and analysts
Leave scraps of lunch behind as they return
To their glass castles, having enjoyed the sun
And the fashionable promenade
Of trim sailboats on the blue, carefree bay.
For these slim, pretty girls and prosperous men,
There is romance in faraway sights
Whose names are crisply spelled on passing ships;
They see the distant mirage, cities of gold

That sparkle beyond the horizon, yet here
The scuttling wharf rat is invisible.

But the bay is not always benign and blue—
In reflecting a darkened sky, it becomes
The grey-green shade of serpentine, the crumbling,
Faulted rock that underlies the nearby hills.
The August breeze that ripples the skirt
Around that girl's bronzed, untouchable legs,
Tousles her sun-bleached hair, and turns
The smooth sailboat on its majestic wings,
In December can lash the underground man
And drive him to the shadow of a doorway.
There, in wakeful hibernation, he burrows
For hours, waiting for the wind to blow itself out
Before his own dim flame flickers and fails.

One by one, the old wooden piers burn down.
And Progress encroaches on the habitat
Of this rough, scavenging beast
That slouches its way in narrowing circles
Toward a carcass already picked clean.

Charms

Jonathan London

Hot. Hot enough to kill. One good thing though, about this heat: it draws out the pine scent, the resins, the sap, like blood from a wound.

But the dust! We career through a ball of it, blind as bats, sweat running in rivulets down our dust-caked bodies.

We've spent the day on the river, the south fork of the Yuba, foothills of the Sierra. All day, cool plunges to slake the body's thirst for reprieve from the heat, which rose in slabs as palpable as granite and slammed us down, the sun's hammer pounding even through the river willow's thin shade. All day, we watched as the crystal pools grew murky from our mad churnings to douse the fires smoldering inside us.

Now the sun is completing its wide arc, and the heat's just showing signs of tapering off, and what we need now more than anything is to eat. Have you ever driven shrouded in dust up steep, potholed dirt roads in the backcountry, with a seven-month-old boy strapped in the back wailing bloody murder and his four-year-old brother whining, "I'm *hungry*," and your own belly burbling like bad plumbing and your wife saying, "This certainly isn't my idea of a nice, relaxing vacation away from everything" —have you?

Feeling uneasy, fearing that in this crowded season our campsite might have been invaded and occupied, we crunch past the sign announcing entrance to the campground, follow the figure eight, and make the sharp turn to the left up the rutted drive to our spot.

There he is: the invader. "Shit!" I hiss, yanking on the hand brake and leaving the motor idling. Sprawled atop our picnic table, hand clutching a beer can, is a scraggly man whose sunken cheeks and eyes and ratty hair spark the image of another man who'd once invaded our space. (Years ago, we'd left our house in the care of a housesitter for three weeks. A student at the California School of Herbal Studies, she'd been recommended by the school's owner and inspiration, a friend of ours. But upon our return, we were greeted by not just the sitter but a pack of kids and her estranged husband, a man who in looks and aspect could have been the double of the man now seated before us.)

"What are you doing here?" I ask, my voice sharpened with hunger and outrage, my sunburned elbow jutting out my window. *The house was a shambles. The garden and house plants dead or dying. Grease coated the frying pan on the kitchen stove, just as scum coated the bathroom sink.*

"Hey, ho! Juz-second, man, this my place here—"

"Fuck it is! Don't ya see our tent over there, our stuff everywhere?" *His hair clogged the bathtub drain.*

"Hey, man, hold on now, I ain't blind. I seen your tent, but I been here for two days, man. Left my stuff here, come back and it's gone." He lifts the can to his lips and swallows, his pointy Adam's apple jerking up and down.

Sure, I'm thinking. "What kind of stuff?" I say. "There was nothing here when we got here this morning."

"Big blue ice chest. Left it right here on this here picnic table. About six this mornin', took off for the day, come back and it ain't here. Someone musta swiped it. You haven't seen a big blue ice chest now have you?"

The guy's so see-through I could scream. I rev my engine, I say, "Look. We got here and there was nothing here and now we want our campsite so we can cook some dinner and eat. Don't you see we've got a crying baby here?" *I rounded him and his scabby family up and ushered them to their van, a big old rusty job just like the one parked behind this joker now.*

He still hasn't budged. He just sits there, all sinewy muscles and veins snaking all over him, wild hair and wild eyes, scraggly Fu-Manchu and patchy black beard, bad teeth and undoubtedly bad breath. Looks like a burnt-out biker. No ape hangers to hang onto, just an empty beer can crumpling in his fist. He shrugs and stares back at me. In this growing gloom of long pine shadows, I can't tell if he's grinning or leering or what. It's a Mexican standoff.

"I hear where you're at, bro, and hell, I mean, sure, I ain't kicking you out; there's room for us all."

"Hell there is! Now I want you out of here. I got kids here and we still got to chop wood and make a fire and cook some dinner and it's almost dark. We came all this way up here to get away, not to share our space with others." *Before they could leave, I gathered the three huge black plastic bags overflowing with garbage—their garbage—and heaped them on their laps. I felt a little sorry for their oldest daughter—a sweet-seeming girl of maybe ten, lost behind big brown eyes and a tangle of hair. Almost pretty in her long hippie dress and dirty-faced purity. She had said she loved our dogs and was going to miss them.* The engine's still purring and Shane's still squalling and Marie's got her hand on my leg but she still hasn't said anything, except to Josh, agitating in the back seat but otherwise uncharacteristically quiet, witnessing what must be to him a strange confrontation between his daddy and a stranger.

"Yeah, I hear where you're coming from, man, but the BLM busted me before for juz crashing in my van 'longside the road, so I juz need a place to park and sleep and I won't be no trouble atall."

I shake my head and point my finger at him. "You're leaving *now*," I tell him. I'm a little afraid of those eyes of his I can't really see, sunk deep in those holes, and though his voice is friendly enough, that knife sheathed at his hip might be used for more than whittling and peeling apples. "There was an empty campsite, number 4 it was, wasn't it, Marie? when we got here. Whatever. You got wheels and you're on your own and I'm sure you'll make out just fine." *When their van full of kids and garbage pulled out, I turned to my wife and said, "The debris of the sixties," and shook my head, as if for the first time disappointed with the results of that experiment of a generation of which I'd been a part.*

He stares at me, and the tip of his tongue jabs out, flicks his lip. Then he tosses his crushed can through his van window, slaps the tops of his thighs, dust poofing up, tips forward, slouches off the table, and climbs into his van. "Right," he says, muttering something I can't catch. Slams his door and fires up his old heap of rust and eases down the cut through the pine and manzanita into the dark. He waves, or flips me the bird, I can't tell which. *And it wasn't until later that we discovered all our best clothes had been ripped off: Marie's alpaca shawl and my alpaca sweater from Puno, on Lake Titicaca, Josh's beautiful, hand-woven, red cap from Afghanistan, a couple of dresses, other things. Neighbors told us that all kinds of ragtag folk had been in and out of our house, crashing there, throwing parties, cleaning out our cupboards, and generally wreaking havoc. And the unpaid bills run up on the telephone! Calls from Colorado billed to our number. And he'd been living out there. His voice false in denying it, later, when I caught up with him and demanded the thirty-five bucks he owed. False, like this character and his "blue ice chest." "It's cool." That's all he could say when I'd placed the garbage on his lap, as if enacting a symbolic gesture. "It's cool." Saying it, but saying it with a menacing smile.*

I turn the key in the ignition, and our wagon shutters into silence. Shane has stopped his wailing, and we just sit there, listening to nothing, to everything.

Out the window I notice a Miller can doubled over beneath the picnic bench, like a man gut-punched, his breath knocked out.

I turn and see that Shane's fast asleep, held from toppling forward by the buckle in his carseat, his fuzzy head dangling like a dead man's. Marie starts to say something, but I'm already out the door and marching up the narrow path to the neighboring campsite.

"Howdy," I say, coming up to a tall, skinny, freckled woman with silky brown hair clear to her ass. Attractive from a distance, close up she is obviously frazzled. She's putting something on the picnic table for her little ones, who are all sitting around waiting with spoons and forks in their fists. No man around, just tents—three of them, two pup tents and a family-sized dome, and lots of trikes and bikes and toys and stuff. Looks like she's pitched camp here for the duration. Clothes hung up on lines. Pots and pans everywhere.

She just looks at me, then ladles out watery stew into yellow plastic bowls.

"I'm your new neighbor down there, and this asshole, uh, excuse me," I stop myself, seeing as how all those kids are watching me. "This guy down there *claimed* it was his campsite—course I don't believe it for a minute..."

"Yeah, he's been there two, three days now," she tells me in a very mellow voice. "Always left a big blue ice chest to let people know the place was taken. Says someone stole it today. Poor guy, it was all he had."

Back at our campsite, I feel like shit. But hell, what could I have done? What would you have done? Night falling and two screaming kids. Starving. Our tent already set up and sleeping bags rolled out. We would've had to strike camp and drive off into the dark and find another campground and *then* make a fire and cook some dinner. It would have been midnight before we filled our bellies and got tucked in.

But still...

I've unlashed from the rooftop carrier the stash of deadfall madrone and pine limbs I'd scored on the roadside, and kindled a good fire. Potatoes wrapped in tinfoil tucked deep among the coals, up against the hot stones. Corn wrapped in tinfoil sizzling in butter and chips of fresh garlic. Steaks splattering juice on the grill, balanced precariously on stones, grill lines striping the succulent meat. Josh is out searching for sticks to roast marshmallows afterwards. I can see him out there flashing the light, hear him singing in the dark—"Oh-h-h I'm so hungry I could eat a tree of fire, I could eat a giant..." Marie slides her short-legged lounge chair up to the fire, sits down, and slips her left tit out. Shane, cradled in her arm, is fastened to it in no time flat, sucking rapturously, his eyes rolling back in ecstasy, his tiny hands gripping and releasing like cat paws, his fat little baby foot kicking.

I reach for the wine, pull the protruding cork with my teeth, drink. "Ah, zin," I say, smacking my lips. "Want some?" I hold out the bottle of red wine, like an offering.

"Not now. Later, thanks." She's gazing down at our baby, stroking his hair, which stands straight up, like a punk's.

"You were a bit aggressive," she says, not looking up.

"Nazi pig, huh? Yeah,...well, I was being one firm daddy—"

"Hard. You were like a reformed alcoholic. I think you saw yourself, your past, in him."

Her words hit some nail in me, make me ring with panic. Just a moment of panic, confusion. Recognition. I want to deny it and agree with her at the same instant. Can't get a word out.

"When I met you, you were living like him. No, you had less than him. Just a pack on your back." (I'd been on the road almost two years, bumming aimlessly around the country, down through Mexico and Central America, up to Canada, where we'd met, stuck on the same on-ramp in the rain, heading East. We hooked up, and when we arrived at her door in Montreal, she said, "Hi, Mama. I've brought a friend home.") "After Suella left you, you depended on friends, and strangers, for food. A place to sleep. You had a way of showing up on people's doorsteps just in time for supper."

"I never lied," I say—I don't know why.

157

"He wasn't lying."

"No."

"You've changed."

"I guess."

"Of course, you had your charms."

"I had luck and good looks."

"Luck, yes."

"Charms."

Makes me feel like a goddam yuppie. No, not quite. I can't afford to be a yuppie. Perhaps that's just another name for people who have feelings that can't be named.

I poke the fire and wonder about him, out there in the night. Maybe no money. Maybe no place to go. Homeless. Some sparks flit and rise up and get lost in the stars.

After a hot day, there's a chill coming on. I crouch closer to the fire for warmth.

"I found one!" Josh shouts, running up, kicking dust and pine cones, panting. I fish out my Swiss Army knife from my hip pocket and whittle the tip of his stick to a sharp point for spearing marshmallows. Shane, his mouth dribbling milk, lifts his head and peeks at me, a smile blooming his face, like a radiant flower. Marie, fire glowing in her dark brown eyes, reaches out toward me, and the wine, and says, "Hon', I'm ready now."

I pass her the bottle and listen, turning my head toward the dark. There's a car out there, or a van. I can hear it. Seems to be coming our way. Its high beams sweep the sugar pines overhead, igniting the branches for a moment, the needles shining. My heart stops, my breath. Then the lights, with the low roar behind them, move on, drilling twin holes into the dark.

Marie hands me the bottle. I grasp it, averting my eyes, still listening, and take a deep slug.

I just want to be able to feel good about myself.

State Park Homeless

Daniel Lindley

A great deal of attention has been paid to the urban homeless over the past few years. Partly, this is because the great media duchies are in the cities, where reporters and editors cross paths with people who live in the streets and flophouses. Much less attention has been given to people in the smaller towns and countryside who have no roofs over their heads, though social services in these places tend to be limited, and locals are less tolerant of poor strangers.

So when I read in a local newspaper that a lot of people had begun living in a state park in the Santa Cruz mountains, and that they were being threatened with eviction, I thought it would be worth a story. Henry Cowell State Park is not especially remote. It's an easy drive from San Jose or Santa Cruz. But it is definitely rural, encompassing thousands of acres of sparsely forested mountains thick with bay laurel, madrone, and redwoods.

The story had a certain appeal to me as a free-lance journalist. Beyond the obvious but crucial fact that the homeless were a hot topic at the time (it was the winter of 1986) and I knew I could find a home for the article, I felt a certain affinity. Staff reporters at newspapers and TV stations take financial, legal, and emotional shelter in the institutions that employ them. Free-lancers are journalism's homeless, floating from story to story, publication to publication, usually neglected or even despised, summoned to do a quick odd job or piece of dirty work for very little money.

So I made a few calls. I lined up a likely buyer in Pacific News Service, a wire service usually called left-liberal. Ten or twenty years ago the fashionable word was "radical." You never hear things referred to as right-conservative, but I guess that's a sign of the times. I also scheduled an interview with Gerald Fialho, the head of the regional state park district.

I met him a few days later. Sheets of rain were lashing across the narrow, twisted road that snaked up to park headquarters. I expected Fialho to be ensconced in some quaint cottage, converted into an office yet brimming with rusticity. What greeted me was a squat, boxlike structure that had all the charm of a Pizza Hut. Inside, it was a standard-issue state government office: lots of glass, linoleum, imitation wood grain, and listless browns and greens, as if a psychologist-consultant hired years ago by a forgotten state commission had determined that these colors would be least likely to agitate any potentially contumacious petitioners who might find their way to such a place.

Fialho was a twenty-eight-year veteran of the department and had the easygoing style of a man accustomed to dealing with the public in all its multifarious forms and expressions on state lands. He had graying hair and an incipient pot, and I expected his appraisal of the situation, in the manner of most bureaucrats, to be reticent and bland.

What did he expect of me? Perhaps he would be even more stolid than I expected, reluctant to discharge tidbits to a journalist carrion bird come to pick over a fresh corpse, an opinion an appreciable share of the public holds of reporters. Plenty of people have made clear to me their conviction that journalists make their living off the suffering and misfortune of others. At times, interviewing weeping relatives of the dead, I have thought them right. But taken to its logical conclusion, that charge could be laid against most of the population, from doctors and lawyers and cops and real estate agents down to loan sharks and common thieves. People live off each other, call it parasitism or symbiosis or what you will. Journalists at least are supposed to get at the truth, and they succeed often enough to provide some excuse for their grisly inquiries. Would it be better to report only happy news, leaving readers to speculate about the world's victims or simply to ignore them?

After we had exchanged pleasantries, Fialho laid out the facts. In the past year or so, a change had come to his jurisdiction. Increasingly, people with nowhere else to stay were moving into his campground. It was cheap. Up to eight people could share a campsite, splitting the nightly fee of six dollars. It was safe, quiet, and they could avail themselves of facilities like barbecue pits, toilets, and running water.

160

These people came from all walks of life and from all over the country, Fialho said. Some were just "free spirits," lured by the popular image of California beaches and sunshine, and had no intention of supporting themselves. A few families used the park campgrounds, though the majority of homeless campers were individuals or couples. Many came from the depressed farm belt or the Pacific Northwest, where the forest products industry was in a slump. They had heard that there were jobs in California, but what they had not heard was that these usually were low-paying jobs. Combined with the state's high real estate prices and rents, this meant they could not afford to live anywhere. Many of these people were commuting between the park and their jobs in San Jose or Santa Cruz.

So attractive were the park's amenities, compared with the few other alternatives in Santa Cruz—sleeping in a chronically over-crowded shelter or under a bridge by the river or curled up in front of the library or various storefronts—that the numbers finding their way here had snowballed. In all but the summer months, 80 percent of the people in the park had nowhere else to stay.

This swelling number of resident campers had caused no particular problem for Fialho or his staff. Though impoverished, the new arrivals, by their nearly constant presence, tended to discourage sneak thieves. Now and then some petty larceny was reported, but no more on average than in the past, or among the park population as a whole.

But by their mere presence, they had antagonized the more traditional kind of camper, which is why they were being threatened with eviction. Most of the complaints came from people who drive those monstrous twenty- and thirty-foot-long trailers, which visitors from other countries sometimes mistake for public transportation.

Fialho pulled a sheaf of letters out of a file cabinet. These people had several beefs. For one thing, the homeless were getting a "corner" on the campsites, especially on busy weekends in the spring and fall. There were complaints about noise, trash, music, people setting up couches in their campsites, and gripes from those who had driven long distances only to be turned away at Henry Cowell's gates because the campground was full. One complaint cited a man who not only lived in the park but made his living there, fixing transmissions. I could agree that a transmission shop certainly was a far cry

161

from a wilderness experience, but the rest of the aesthetic question certainly was open to debate. Had some arbiter of good taste decreed that a beige, twenty-five-foot Winnebago bristling with dirt bikes, TV antennae, metal barbecues, and plastic coolers is any less ugly than the aforementioned scars upon the campground?

In this case, clout decided the issue. All campers were equal, though some more than others. Winnebago owners are more likely to vote and complain than the homeless, and as a result of all the letters and complaints, the Parks Department had proposed a thirty-day-per-year limit on stays at each campground in the system. This, it was hoped, would drive out the homeless. Fialho, as I expected, was noncommittal about the proposal, a man caught between warring factions, though he and his fellow parks employees seemed sympathetic to the homeless. As we were discussing the RV owners' complaints, a tall, blond ranger appeared in the doorway. "The homeless don't particularly like the Winnebagos with their generators," he pointed out in an almost defensive tone.

I drove over to the campground as the rain began to taper off. It was the middle of the day and not many campers were around. Of several score campsites it appeared that half a dozen were in use. The scene was vaguely depressing, in concert with the weather. Blue plastic tarps seemed to litter the woods. They covered possessions and wood and were strung along clotheslines between saplings as makeshift tents. I parked my car and began ambling along the campground loop.

All the campsites in use appeared to be occupied by the poor. The closest thing to a Winnebago was a beat-up old pickup truck. On its back a camper shell listed oddly. The owner, a large, middle-aged black man, was getting out of the cab, so I walked up and introduced myself. We talked for a few minutes, he protesting without being prodded that he was only there for a holiday.

"I'm no bum," he explained. "I've been working all my life. I'm waiting for a phone call to get this job. These guys don't want to work." He pointed to a raucous crowd of young people who were drinking and talking about the best ways to get government freebies.

I thought he was lying for social reasons, to separate himself from the neighbors he considered riffraff. Or perhaps he thought I was some sort of state official, come undercover to roust out the poor. The tone of his voice, his claim that he owned a house in Santa Cruz, and the condition of his camper made it unlikely that he was there for a few days' vacation. I wished him well as he again insisted he had a job and a house.

I next approached a faded, old, white station wagon. A sallow woman was curled up asleep in the back. A pale, thin man who looked to be in his mid-thirties was sitting up in the driver's seat, his head tipped back as if he had pulled off to the side of the road for a nap. But his eyes were wide open, though partly concealed by a shock of dark hair that fell across his forehead.

I knocked tentatively on his window. He didn't seem to want to open it, but finally relented a little, rolling it down an inch. I explained my mission. "Go away," he said, scowling. "I don't want to talk."

He didn't look amenable to persuasion. Anyway, one thing a reporter learns is that in most cases, there are other sources...even in this nearly deserted spot, in a gray-green mist under a canopy of redwoods.

I followed a wisp of smoke to its source. A youngish man in blue jeans was squatting like an Indian on the damp forest floor, nursing along a pathetic little fire with damp pine needles and shards of kindling. When I introduced myself, he motioned to me to sit on a log.

His name was Robert Farrell and he was forty-three years old. He and his brother, who had gone to town for groceries, had been sharing a small domed tent here for a few weeks. He told me his story as he poked at the fire with a stick. He had lost his job in Silicon Valley several months ago. For a while he had stayed on at his apartment, but his unemployment check of $137 hadn't been enough to cover rent and other necessities. He moved to a cheap hotel in downtown San Jose but still came up short. When he was thrown out, he drifted to a homeless shelter in San Francisco. He finally got fed up with conditions there, which included general filth and a case of lice, so he linked up with his brother, also newly unemployed, and they drove down to Henry Cowell.

How long did they plan to stay? A few months, maybe. Had he heard of the thirty-day limit? Yes. He shook his head. "I don't know where there's any other place to stay."

There was little left to say. What could I do but wish him luck? He nodded sadly. Soon the rain began to fall again, and as I walked away I looked back and saw him feeding more wet pine needles to the listless fire. I walked the rest of the campground, but there was no one left to interview. Even the drinking party had vanished.

In the next few days I called some of the parks people Fialho had mentioned who were having similar problems in other parts of the state. About half a dozen other parks were reporting friction between homeless people and vacationers. Most of the trouble spots were at beaches in Southern California. "Some of these people are just down and out, don't have money, and are obviously decent folks," said the supervisor of one southern district. "The ones who are problems are doing it just because it's cheap. They know how to work the system, and they spend the rest on drugs and alcohol."

His jurisdiction included San Clemente State Beach, a short walk along the coast from the estate once known as the Western White House when Richard Nixon owned it. Houses in the area are worth a million dollars or more. But the wealthy homeowners weren't the ones complaining. Again, it was the middle-class Winnebago set who was unhappy.

It made sense in a strange way. The rich, after all, could retreat into the confines of their gardens and mansions if the sight of poverty displeased them. The middle class were left on the beach to fight with the poor over the scraps left for them by the state. The whole situation began to seem tawdry and pathetic. Yet who could blame these Winnebago people, really, most of them hard working, or retired after a lifetime of struggle? They'd probably spent their life savings buying and fueling those gargantuan contraptions.

And certainly, no one could blame the homeless for being there. They had nowhere else to go, no place, at least, where they could live with a few shreds of dignity and enjoyment.

I wrote the story and it got picked up by a lot of newspapers, as best I could make out from PNS's erratic clipping service. As I said earlier, the homeless were hot then. And the image of Winnebago people finding down-and-outs in their vacation sites was a good hook.

There remains the question of the story's effect. The fact is that most pieces of journalism fall into some dark recess of the public consciousness, there to be crowded out by sit-coms, beer and hamburger commercials, and worries about jobs and mortgages and traffic jams and a thousand other things. The power of the press is overrated most often by the press itself.

The thirty-day limit was adopted statewide that summer. It was almost completely successful in its design to drive the homeless out of the parks, though a few got around the new rule by moving from park to park.

I went back to Henry Cowell a few days ago. It had been an unusually dry winter, and the forest floor looked like tinder. The sun beat down, birds warbled, the redwoods creaked in a northwesterly breeze. I saw no blue tarps, jalopies, or painted buses. They had been replaced by four or five mammoth RVs plus a couple of tents set next to Japanese cars of recent vintage. Two old guys in baseball caps and carrying metal detectors disappeared down a forest trail. Otherwise the place seemed deserted. The homeless were gone, scattered as if by the wind that rustled the old redwoods.

A Few Days Before Christmas, San Francisco, 1986

Craig Van Riper

Yellow papers in the alley cover the spoiled
food, the dead men, silent and sleeping.
More street people ceased their suffering
this year than in any other year
in the history of this shaking town.
What was it the newsbrief said today,
eighty-five? fifty-eight? We keep the exact
number in the daily death ledger;
for we count only the dead, the stiff
limbs lying beside broken bottles of Night Train,
Thunderbird. Those alive are left
unaccounted for, trembling and invisible.
When we see their ghost figures
we ask, "Isn't it sad?" and look
the other way. But our turned heads
cannot shield us from their words, their cries:
guilt oozes through our pores
like clammy beads of sweat. And still
we force our minds to forget
the homeless piles by the road, think
pleasant thoughts and pick up our pace.

The Sin

Eric Lukacs

It is cold this morning. A fog blankets the valley, hides the mountains and sun. In the oak tree, whose branches overhang my bedroom,
crested jays pick for morsels of fat insects; the refuse of their search
drops heavily on my roof.

Grey squirrels have begun the fall harvest. I count the acorns that
fall upon the taut skin of the roof and roll, shingle by shingle, down
the sloping side, splashing into the sea of leaves below my window.
In the racket of such abundance, I admit the futility of further rest.

Later, I stand on the balcony with my hands wrapped tightly
around a cup of coffee. I watch the fattened birds fly towards the
river, dispersing the fog with the wind of their wings and self-satisfied
screeches. Pale sunlight fills the valley, streaming through the last
flimsy wisps of mist. Woodsmoke scents the air.

I am in hiding. I came from the south, from the sprawling
behemoth that is Los Angeles: a place that consumes whole cities
and towns, regurgitating them as faceless reincarnations, enslaving
them in the pall of its brown, polluted breath. The city, engorged
with its minions, is stopped only by the natural boundary of the sea.
There, where the winds and tides battle the onslaught of crazed
technology, a thin line of deteriorating livability is established. I
have turned from that place in retreat from the face of vacant,
hopeless desperation.

Beyond the stretch limousines, the comings and goings of
presidents and popes, beneath the sweep of spotlights, just there,
where the light refracts in the gold sequined gown blinding us with
its glare, is the sin of America. This stain on the soul of the land is
in the grime-soiled faces of thousands upon thousands of poor and
homeless.

I speak of sin in the sense of aberration, something horrifyingly opposed to nature, an infestation that causes the death of spirit. In a society whose scope of wealth and power has no equal in history, the homeless are our sin and shame.

Perhaps as nowhere else in this country, Los Angeles bears grim witness to our fall from grace. The semi-arid environment provides a margin of survivability when one's home is the hollow of a building, the underpass of a freeway, or the hedge in front of a bank. With wicked irony, whole neighborhoods spring up in parking lots, based on the architecture of the refrigerator carton.

Here the less intimidated of our citizenry see fit to rob and plunder the poor, taking what meager goods they might have accumulated in the all too brief hours of daylight. Their wounds fester with infection, while our medical centers shun them or bleed them further with bureaucratic blades of insensitivity. All the while the children of these cardboard towns make their hungry way through the tears of their mothers' despair.

But the darkest stain of all is that we have seen fit to pilfer the resources of our mental institutions and release their charges onto the streets. I close my eyes and I can see them haunting the streets, clothed in the costumes of their deluded visions, wheeling possession-laden shopping carts through the corridors of the street. I see them in endless dialogue with their own reflections that appear in the smokey glass of our venerable institutions of commerce.

Lest I appear too self-righteous in my condemnation, I am certainly not without guilt. I have gone to great lengths to avoid imminent meetings with the destitute by strategically crossing streets or carefully marking my path to avoid their gathering places. Out of sight, out of mind.

In his satiric essay "A Modest Proposal," Jonathan Swift suggests that in order to rid ourselves of the poor we begin to cannibalize them. I would contend that we have accepted his proposition, for we have skewered them on our indifference, masticated them with our arrogance, and digested them in the acidic juice of our greed.

But the worst insult is to ourselves as people: we have allowed ourselves to be manipulated by the wielders of economic power in this country. They have used poverty to intimidate and coerce us into silent complicity with a self-serving, lopsided system of distribution, lest we become one of "them"—the poor, the homeless, the abandoned. Fear is the great progenitor of this sin.

168

This, then, is the real aberration: we have all agreed to avert our eyes, to slip our blinders in place and bless our masters for the tidbits thrown our way as we chase the golden carrot they dangle before our faces.

So I stand in my retreat. The smell of wet grass fills the air, trees in sunlight sparkle on the rolling hillsides. The early chill has subsided, and I can see the last flowers of summer in the garden below. Later today the plants will be watered. When the cat cries it will be fed, and as I stand, watching it eat, I will pretend I am a decent man.

Lullaby

David Joseph

Mama, Mama,
When can I eat?

Hush up. Hush up.
You'll get no food today.
Your daddy got no pay.

Mama, Mama,
Why are we on the street?

Hush up. Hush up.
We can live in a tent.
The landlord wanted rent.

Mama, Mama,
Why can't I sleep?

Shut your eyes and dream
of a snorting mare
and its fixed stare.

Rescue Mission

Jay Chambers

No one looked rescued to me
staggering in under a blue neon cross
all mumbly, prickle-faced and nappy haired.
Men mostly,
uniformed by some weird coincidence
in navy-blue knit caps and green army surplus jackets.
A dozen snarling strays in a push-and-shove soup line
with backs to the red-haired girl singing hymns on the stage.
And then, there was pointed Mrs. Peale, sanctified and satisfied,
who steadied her ladle over quivering bowls
by fixing her thin lips into an awry pose.
She knows the choking reek of mildewed magazines, stale sweat,
and, of course, spirits (she is inoculated to nausea).
Finally a retired army captain preached in a loud drone,
after which some of the sinners cried and got saved again.
Then everyone compared the coffee to battery acid, or tar, or
worse, and out the door they fell, into the concrete ocean,
to be rescued again tomorrow.

For Sarah

Ellis Ovesen

i showed you my precious shell
collection,
blonde little two-year-
old
with Shirley Temple
curls...

living with your mom and
dad
in a battered car on the
beach
until daddy can find
work...

your potty chair under a
bush
your shower with your
daddy
your bed in the back seat at night
with your parents...

you carefully picked up the
shells
but they crushed in your baby
fingers
your muscles not yet ready for the
fragility of shells...

completely did i forgive
you
when you placed a yellow
dandelion
in my pocket as you
left...

Papa Fritz

Delores Goodrick Beggs

The old man struggled to push the heavy wooden cart up the last part of the incline. White, straggly hair topped a body thin and bent with age; the emphysema curve of his back was emphasized because he had lowered his head between reedy arms to throw the whole of his weary weight into the final push up the hill.

One foot slipped on a damp cobblestone, and he braced, quickly shifting his weight to the secure leg, feeling beneath him for solid footing on the side that had lost traction. The streets of San Miguel were notoriously steep and damp year round, and especially bad now in the rainy season. He still had to go down the other side and find a place to ford the stream, created by yesterday's rains because of the lack of drainage systems, before he could find a safe place to sleep tonight.

Along the narrow street were brilliant splashes of the large flowers that grew profusely in the rich soil, no more vibrant than the old man's secondhand outfit of conflicting patterns and clashing colors. One glance at him and his old cartful of possessions, covered now with a ragged quilt as protection against a sudden drizzle, showed he was a man of the streets.

He found a dry spot to place his foot and began the slow uphill push again, step by dogged step, finally reaching the top and a level resting place, a parklike area, empty except for a young girl playing by the bushes at the far end. He locked the cart wheels and sagged down in relief on the single, splintery bench.

The girl suddenly stood before him, her small, warm hand reaching for his knobby, leathery one. Holding it firmly, she smiled. "I'm Ginna. What's your name?"

He bared his teeth. A twisted, black space where three were missing lent him a sinister look that had proven effective in ridding him of unwanted intruders. For years now he had lived on the fringe of life, and he preferred to remain there, having no desire to be pulled again into the mainstream, however fleetingly.

But Ginna chose to ignore the black, twisted, empty side of his mouth. She gazed intently into his eyes, pulling impatiently at his hand. "Don't you have a name?" she asked again.

"I've been called Papa Fritz." The words brought back memory. Nan, dying. Andrea, warm and loving. *"Come home with me, Papa Fritz. I've got a place for you."* He'd gone, and it had been fine, at first. Then it became a strain, never Andrea's fault, she was a good girl always, but Papa Fritz watched her become thin and tired, and often was awakened by arguing voices that reached his room late at night. One day, Papa Fritz looked at Andrea's peaked face, packed his bag, and said goodbye to his stepdaughter. Andrea kissed him lovingly; tears blurred her violet eyes, so much like Nan's had been, but she didn't try to stop him. He'd been traveling the streets ever since, first with his brown cloth bag, and later, as things accumulated during his travels, with the cart. Until now, he'd been alone.

Ginna tugged at his hand, bringing him back to the present. "Will you help me, Papa Fritz? Over there? Come and see."

He got slowly to his feet, his tired muscles having stiffened. Ginna dropped his hand and skipped ahead, stopping where a profusion of red and yellow tulips surrounded a tree.

"Don't scare it," she whispered, and knelt to carefully part the tulips. "I think it's hurt, Papa Fritz. Can you help it?"

The bird panicked and flailed its good wing, flopping itself onto its other side.

"Here now, come to Papa Fritz," the old man cooed, leaning past the girl to scoop up the frightened bird, sheltering it in his hands and stroking it gently. When it was still, he examined it. The wing was almost certainly broken, but perhaps would heal with care.

"Will it be all right, Papa Fritz?" Ginna was worried.

"I'll take care of it, splint the wing, feed it. It'll be fine in no time at all."

"I'm so glad!" she cried, relieved, then clapped a hand over her mouth in dismay as the bird started again. When Papa Fritz had the bird quiet once more, Ginna said, "Don't you think she should have a name? What shall we call her?"

Papa Fritz looked down at the tulip bed. "How about Tuli?"

174

"I like that," Ginna said, her eyes big with pleasure. "And I'll come every day and help you care for her."

"No."

"But I want to help. I found her," Ginna insisted.

"We won't be here. We'll be moving on, Ginna."

"But where, Papa Fritz? I'll get Mama to bring me."

"No, Ginna. Leave Tuli to me." His tone was gentle, and final. Like when he had told Andrea he was leaving.

Ginna eyed him rebelliously. He was talking like her daddy when he wanted a subject dropped. "Do you have a little girl, Papa Fritz?"

The question caught him unaware. "Well, yes, Ginna. A step-daughter. But she's grown now, and has a family of her own."

"Does she know where you are?"

He was nonplussed at the girl's perceptiveness, and had no ready answer.

In the distance, a woman's voice was calling Ginna.

"My mother's calling," Ginna said. "I have to go. I'll leave Tuli with you, Papa Fritz. She likes you and she's scared of me. But if you were my papa, I'd want to know where you were, even if I was grown up!" She cast a final look at the hurt pigeon, held securely in Papa Fritz's arms, and ran home.

Papa Fritz carried the injured bird back to his cart and wrapped it in an old towel, so only the head peered out.

"Eh, Tuli, you think she's right? Should we go back to Andrea?" He released the wheels of the cart and paused, considering. The bird began struggling in its wrappings, and he stroked it to calm it.

"Nice Tuli," he crooned, "Never mind. I'll look after you. Andrea doesn't need us. We'll go down and ford the stream, then I'll find us a nice safe place to spend the night."

Papa Fritz began pushing the heavy cart, talking to the bird all the while. Already, he was planning how to get bread crumbs to keep his Tuli fed.

What it is

Raymond Thompson

It is not
just waking on rooftops
above dreamed Victorian houses
stunned by morning
or playing chess in public places
measuring time by the sun
while dreading the oncoming night
nor is it the relentless soup lines
leading to doubt

It is not just
Scrabble spelling a way
out of wounded weather
and never getting 86ed
from all-night alleys

It is more about
the driver's questions
about my lost ticket perhaps
than how my name was left off
some list
already turned in
or in being unable to recall
on what exact yesterday
I got confused in the fog

on the way
to some party
where she might have been

And still all pasts imagined
like oceans of joys unattained
dance like the gemmy tips of waves
tantalizing the possible
and end up
trickling to the now

this moment hangs
like a drop
of water
over
undone dishes

I walk the city
cut thru backyards
looking
for the right papers
I need to get in order
not to be held accountable

I wander into antique shops
looking for some object
lost a body or two ago

It is more
than digging
a perfect blue bottle
from the earth
like a gem
that was forgotten
and found buried

under old costumes
that gave safe passage
thru wrong neighborhoods
and years

It is nothing
less than terror
waking
at the edge
of
unraveled
calendars

homeless
but for that uncharted place
inside the rain

Wind on Hillegass

Stephen Ronan

The wind lifts the coattail of the black hobo,

    he pulls his bedroll tighter,

    faded colors in hard sunlight.

The wind streams through touched-up green,

    the quixotic vacant lot,

    its sudden shock of grass.

The wind chinks a forlorn bell

    on the porch of no takers,

    over the table of no dice.

The wind snaps red caution flags

    in a neighborhood

    organized against crime.

The wind rattles mummified leaves

    on a bony tree,

    roots buried in private property.

Don't Look at the Dying

Julia Vinograd

Don't look at the dying;
you'll only encourage them.
the homeless, the hungry, the hurting,
they're not really there
and it's not polite to stare.
you're driving your wallet
on the rush-hour freeway
so don't stop for empty pockets
or slow down to look at accidents
or the bogeyman'll get you.
pretty soon the cops'll clear them
all away
anyway,
and your eyes will be safe.
And when you're dying
      (oh yes, you will)
no one will look.

Payloads Into Caseloads:
An Immodest Proposal

Cecile Pineda

It is a melancholy sight for those who must drive their cars, or worse still, walk through the streets of our vast and flourishing metropolises—or for that matter, travel in the country significantly detached from the Capital—to see alleys, roadways, streets, boulevards, even major thoroughfares choked with unending lines of homeless paupers, often with the entire repertoire of their possessions about their persons, packed in shopping carts, three-wheelers, milk crates, shopping bags, garbage disposal sacks, and all other manner of receptacle, taking up passage on sidewalk and gutter, littering the venue of their waiting with discarded cigarette butts, candy wrappers, abandoned newspapers, obsolescent fast-food containers, and the like. And many of them in rags, half-inebriated, some of them doubtless drugged, panhandling each passer-by for nickels and dimes. When they could, all of them would work for an honest livelihood rather than employing their time loitering, begging sustenance for unfed children, not one of whom was in evidence.

Further, I think it has been agreed by all parties that in the present state of the economy, this unholy gathering of persons represents a weighty and intolerable further grievance, interfering with more serious budgetary matters at hand, in particular the security of our sovereign state and the defense thereof. Therefore, if there is anyone who could find out a happy and easy method of enhancing our national position in the world while at the same time serving these unfortunate persons, he could expect to be viewed very much in the light of a national hero.

I have it on good authority from a female lately given to *Social Work* (by which is meant tiresome meddling in the affairs of those less fortunate than oneself) that there is some ungracious talk among the poor and undeserving and their advocates that monies which ought rightfully to have been allocated to them in their misfortune instead have been misappropriated by those members of our Pentagon who (it is universally agreed) are in most dire need of expanding their pitiable armamentum to meet the claims of defending this great Nation.

In putting forward my proposal, therefore, I wish to insist that my intentions are not in any way limited to providing shelter for these aforementioned unfortunates. It is of a much wider scope in that it affects not only those applicants and recipients of welfare, but the preservation of our national sovereignty and of the natural beauty and magnificence of our great cities as well. I therefore propose as follows:

That those long-range missiles—numbering two thousand, already paid for at heavy taxpayer expense—shall immediately on being decommissioned by virtue of the recent Summit Treaty be stripped of their payloads, and that their steel casings be transported forthwith to suitable locations, such as freightyards or stockyards, away from the eye of the public where it might otherwise give offense, so that the poor may be domiciled within them. Deployed horizontally, and given the durability of their materials, their exteriors should be proof against rain, sleet, and snow, and if the poor are properly clustered in suitable density within their interiors, their body warmth will generate enough heat to safely keep them from freezing in summer, and possibly in winter as well. Thus sheltered, they will no longer have to avail themselves of corrugated cardboard (which might valuably be recycled), cluttering subway gratings, offending the sensibilities of every passer-by, particularly in the more wealthy and well-appointed neighborhoods of our cities.

I call upon my readers to envision the ingenuity of such a scheme. Given a housing of roughly two meters in diameter, the poor could be stood vertically by day, three, or possibly four, abreast. Given a cylinder length of upwards of 30 meters, each cylinder could comfortably domicile 360 unfortunates, allowing something equal to a foot for each occupant—front to back—for, given their reduced intake, seldom do the inmates have the opportunity to grow fat. To provide sleeping facilities by night, one need only stretch the inhabitants horizontally end-to-end, in several layers of thickness, thereby providing the ease of warmth and comfort.

If my calculations are correct, within a happily brief time the practice will encourage further weapons dismantlement in the full and satisfied assurance that several trillion of our prime taxpayer dollars can enjoy recyclement in a worthy cause. And with the hastening of weapons decommissioning, even more homeless can be accommodated, and at zero-level taxpayer expense.

There is a further subtlety perhaps not immediately apparent to my scheme. For with the acceleration of missile dismantlement, the nation's economy is certain to be spurred to yet greater heights by the frenzy to get, design, and fabricate ever more complicated conventional weaponry to replace those vast deployments of our more theoretical deterrents. All our citizenry will benefit: there will be a new and vigorous recrudescence of prosperity—in which the homeless will receive no undeserved part, being safely and happily tucked out of sight.

Let me assure those who may inquire, that my proposal is purely without any purpose of self-advancement. For the past twenty years, other than endeavoring to promote this inspired remedy, I have had no source of employment in the defense of my country. Far removed from weapons fabrication or deployment, my efforts have been harmlessly and unprofitably employed in the making of Art, such poor things as books and entertainments for the theatre. I have, by virtue of my singular and unswerving dedication to my various muses, been excluded from the happy category of those who must pay taxes to the state, and have no further end in sight here but for the public Good of my country and the Preservation of its natural landscape.